And Life Lights Up

MOMENTS THAT MATTER

About Alice's other books

Home for Christmas

'Taylor's joy of everything that surrounds the festivities
permeates each page.' *Sunday Business Post*

Do You Remember?

'Magical … Reading the book, I felt a faint ache in my heart … I find
myself longing for those days … This book is important social history …
remembering our past is important. Alice Taylor has given us a handbook
for survival. In fact, it is essential reading.'

Irish Independent

And Time Stood Still

'It's as if she just writes down on the page what she was feeling, you don't
get any sense that there is any filter between you and the writer.'

Arena, RTÉ Radio 1

To School through the Fields

'One of the most richly evocative and moving portraits of
childhood ever written.' *Boston Globe*
'Ireland's Laurie Lee.' *The Observer*

Alice Taylor grew up on a farm in North Cork. There, out in the quiet fields, seeds of joy and mindfulness were planted. Since then she has learnt the importance of being present in each moment to better absorb and enjoy special times as they happen. Even very ordinary experiences may be shot through with rays of delight. But we have to be in the now to enjoy these golden times.

Alice has written many books about country living and the changing face of Ireland. In this book she takes us on a mindful journey through everyday, ordinary living.

OTHER BOOKS
Memoirs:
To School through the Fields
The Village
The Parish
And Time Stood Still
The Gift of a Garden
Do You Remember?
The Women
Tea and Talk
Home for Christmas

Fiction:
The Woman of the House
Across the River
The House of Memories

See the complete list at www.obrien.ie

And Life Lights Up

MOMENTS THAT MATTER

Alice Taylor

Photographs by Emma Byrne

First published 2018 by Brandon,
an imprint of The O'Brien Press
12 Terenure Road East, Rathgar,
Dublin 6, DO6 HD27, Ireland
Tel: +353 1 4923333; Fax: +353 1 4922777
E-mail: books@obrien.ie
Website: www.obrien.ie
The O'Brien Press is a member of Publishing Ireland.

ISBN 978-1-78849-058-0

Printed by L&C Printing Group, Poland.
This book is produced using pulp from managed forests.

Published in:

DUBLIN
UNESCO
City of Literature

Dedication

To Lena
who lights up my life

Contents

Introduction –
Golden Moments

Deep within each one of us is a vein of sacred stillness holding the seeds of our awareness. On special occasions a ray of light beams into this vein and these seeds spring to life, igniting dormant threads of our being. Our inner world lights up and dances in tune with all that surrounds us. We glory in the wonder of being alive. Such moments are golden, rare orchids scattered along the woodland of our lives.

It is for these moments that we scale mountaintops, penetrate the depths, pit ourselves against the might of man and nature, strive to be raised up so that for a few minutes we dance on a higher plane. We are in total harmony with ourselves and with life.

When the moment passes we live in the afterglow of the experience. We walk on, enriched by this secret inner glow because we have flown above and beyond the ordinary. We have danced with life and with our inner being. We are rejuvenated.

Sometimes nature can lay such golden moments out in front of us on a palette of breathtaking beauty. It can happen unexpectedly, out of the blue – and for one brief interlude our world is transformed. On a remote mountain road we may drive slowly around a sharp bend – and there it is, an unbelievably beautiful hidden valley. Nature holds a key to open our windows into wonder. Amazing moments can also be gifted to us by our fellow humans. This happens when genius touches us. We hear it in a beautiful piece of music – for a few magical moments we and the performer dance together. We see it in a beautiful ballet when the ballerina becomes a bird in flight. We read it in a soul-stirring poem where words written thoughtfully allow us to see the world through the eyes of the poet. We see it in an exquisite painting – on the canvas we and the artist are one. These moments can form a link across the decades; the artist may be dead for centuries, but creativity is an invisible bridge across time.

When we are gifted with these rare insights, a ray of radiance encompasses us. It lifts us up and we experience an interlude from ordinary life that infuses us with delight and a positive belief in the greatness of our fellow human beings. We wish that these moments could last forever. But if we mindfully absorb them as they happen we can encapsulate them into the depths of our being where they mould themselves into the fabric of our souls and carry us over the stumbling blocks that may lie ahead.

A horse-trainer friend of mine, who has seen many fallings and risings in his racing career, says about days when he has a winner, 'I don't go to bed at all that night.' He believes in taking the time to absorb the exultation, to lace the magic moment into the fabric of his psyche to help carry him over future crash landings.

We may not all walk in the winner's enclosure or stand on the podium of achievement or raise the cup of victory, but we do all have beautiful moments, special times that can set our inner being aglow and wake us up to the wonder that surrounds us. But we must be there for these experiences and in them. They enrich our lives but can so easily be lost if we are too busy looking in another direction. They can then go by, unappreciated and unnoticed. They just disappear. So it is good to be mindful, to be aware, to observe and savour these special moments, and absorb the joy of them now as they are happening and take them into our soul.

PART 1
Awareness

Cherish the moment as it may
never happen again.

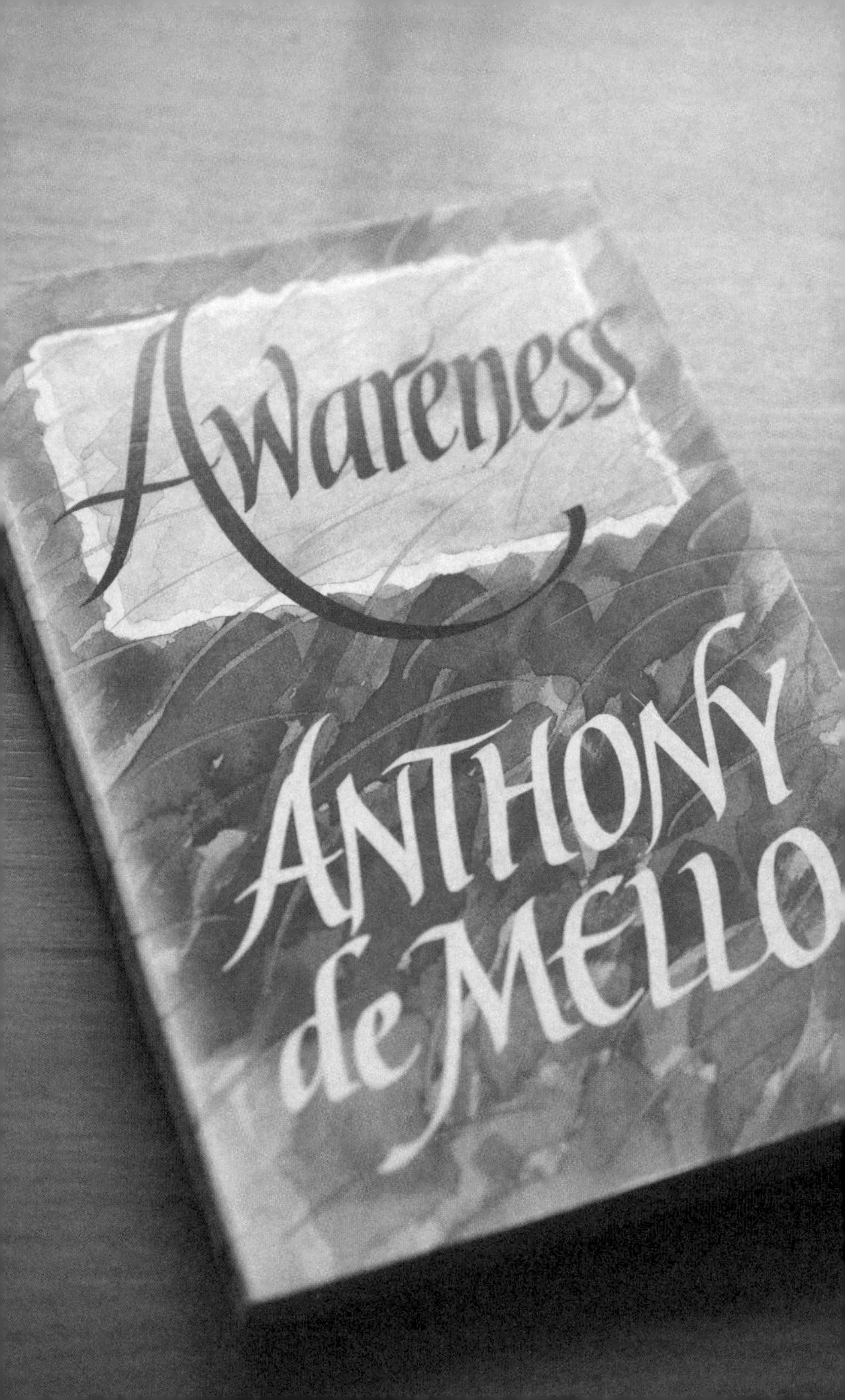
Awareness
ANTHONY
de MELLO

Out of Our Minds

You have been evicted. Your mind has been taken over by the outside world. A demanding army has moved into your head and encamped where you should be. You have moved out and retreated to live at a distance from yourself. You want desperately to come home. To get back into yourself. To live again within yourself. To rest in the peaceful places of your own mind. But that space is occupied. A noisy world has moved in. How did that happen? When did it happen? You have no idea! It must have happened when you were busy doing something else, preoccupied with another project.

This happens to us all. Frequently. But now, how do we get that invading army out? Where to begin? This army in the mind will not easily surrender. This occupying force of noise and confusion has taken up residence and stubbornly refuses to leave. It has decided that this is its territory. It will not be moved. We are lost in confusion.

But we must make some effort! We try confrontation. We try shouting down this inner noise. Talk, talk, talk. But that does not work. More noise only creates more conflict. We simply end up in a worse state. So, confrontation is definitely not the answer. But what is the answer? There has to be an answer.

How about simple silence? Could silence be the answer? Could silence evict the noisy army? Sounds a bit too easy. Would the voices actually move out and allow peace of mind to move in? Worth a try. It could take time for a mental door to quietly open and allow it in. But we must slow down and allow this to happen. Can we slow down? Can we stop?

Our engine has become accustomed to fast-forward living. There is so much to be done. But we are exhausted from rushing. Is it possible to slow down? It *has* to be possible.

What I usually do is sit quietly in silence. Sounds like a simple thing to do. It may sound simple but it is not easy. My mind keeps demanding attention. As the Buddhists say, there is a tree full of chattering monkeys in there in my head. I have already discovered that I cannot out-chatter them because that just stimulates them into more activity. Now I need to find out if a quiet body quietens them down. When the body quietens, will the mind become a quieter place too? Can I introduce a silent quietening into this clamour and noise? Can I find a passive, tranquil silence that simply will not engage with the turmoil?

I sit calmly, patiently, and wait. The monkeys try every stunt in the book to keep the racket going. But then, gradually, they ease off a little. The noisy inner army begins to quieten down and very, very slowly it gives up and reluctantly retreats a little. With no counter-attack there is no battle. Gradually the inner tumult eases and I gain a little ground. Peace slowly creeps in. My mind calms down and the clamour of the world recedes a little more. Quiet spaces open up within. I am slowly able to come back into my own head. I am gradually coming home. Eventually I am home. Quiet. At home.

But how do I stay at home? That is the question. With the best intention in the world, clamour and clutter seep in. That is life. So how do I attempt to ring-fence myself from the chattering monkeys?

Many years ago, when I had a head full of chattering monkeys, a friend gave me a book by Anthony de Mello called *Awareness*. De Mello tried to introduce me to my chattering monkeys. I read the book, but did not get it. Read it again, but still did not get it. Then my friend gave me a de Mello tape to which I listened again and again – and finally I got it. I got to know my monkeys.

Anthony de Mello was an Indian Jesuit who came to the western world and quickly reached the conclusion that we were all crazy. He decided that we were all sleep-walking through our lives in a total lack of awareness. Drastic thinking! People thought that *he* was crazy. In a huge effort to wake us all up he tried to introduce meditation to the West, to introduce it to ordinary people: the butcher, the baker and the candlestick maker! Meditation was not just for monks and enclosed orders, but for ordinary Joe Soaps to get us to wake up and appreciate the here and now. Did he succeed? Not really! He died a young man – but he had sown seeds that are still sprouting up in different corners of the world.

Needs

Give me space
To roll out my mind
So that I can open
Locked corners
Where lost thoughts
Are hidden.
I need time
In a quiet place
To walk around
The outer edges
Of my being,
To pick up
Fragmented pieces,
To put myself
Back together again.

Meeting the
Morning

Ajarring alarm clock jerking you into sudden wakefulness, with an attached radio system shooting every world problem into your mind before you put a foot on the floor, is a brutal introduction to a new day. Your equilibrium is shattered.

When I was one of the jarring alarm-clock brigade there was also the early-morning tear-around looking for lost socks, and the making of school lunches to cope with. Each morning began with this kind of bedlam that hurled me into another day. From there on I was on the treadmill of the daily merry-go-round. Sometimes I wondered could there be another way? Another way to begin the morning that would make a real difference to the day ahead. So very early one morning, before the world woke up, I crept out of bed and down the stairs. Out into the garden. The dawn chorus was just about to begin.

We have a lot to learn from the dawn chorus. On

waking, the birds do not all blast into full song at once. One little voice gives a soft tweet and soon afterwards this is taken up by another, and then another, until, very gently, the wake-up call spreads from one tree to another. With this soft call to meet the new day they all gradually become aware that morning is breaking and so, having begun on a small, delicate note, they slowly raise the volume until, in full chorus, they welcome in the new day. There are no jarring, discordant sounds, just the collective harmony, like a magnificent choir, and yet there is no hidden conductor waving a baton.

In this garden all paths lead to the seat under an old apple tree, and so I sat there and let the surrounding peace seep into my body and mind. A tide of tranquility washed over me, forming a peaceful inner pool.

Into that pool came the memory of another dawn, my first and never-to-be-forgotten awareness of the magic of the dawn when I was eight years old. It was after an all-night vigil, a night up minding the *bonhams*, which was part of the baby-animal caring pattern of our farm life. This was an undertaking that as a young child I was very anxious to experience. I wondered what the world would be like at night when everyone else was asleep.

So I had persuaded my reluctant mother to allow me to stay up with an older sister to mind the *bonhams*.

But the welfare of the baby pigs was way down on my list of priorities. My motivation was a huge curiosity as to how the world functioned at night.

The first change I discovered was the all-encompassing silence. It rested like a blanket over the house and farmyard. Apart from the missing adult voices, the usual farmyard noises too were absent. No squeals from the piggery, no bawling from the calf house, and no quacking from the ducks. All were silent. The only sound breaking that silence was the regular ticking of the kitchen clock. The brass pendulum was easing away the minutes of my precious night.

Outside the kitchen window, hump-shaped bushes strode the ditches and away in the distance the giant Kerry Mountains followed each other like great dark camels along the horizon. Gone were the familiar shapes of the day. Out there the dark night was foreign territory. It was slightly strange and scary.

Beside the turf fire the old sagging sofa offered the comfort of familiarity. I snuggled down into its lumpy depths. My plan was to stay there for just a few minutes, but the arms of Morpheus were irresistible.

When I awoke, the clock was striking four in the morning. Oh no! Some of my precious night had disappeared. It had been sucked down into the realms of sleep.

But while I was down there a change had come

about. Faint splinters of light were filtering in through the windows. Sleepy-eyed, I pawed my way to the door. I found myself in the front porch where a soft fan of light was seeping in under the front door. I rattled the loose brass knob and the door eased open.

Outside was a transformed world. The tip of the red ball of the sun was edging its way over the horizon, shooting arrows of light across the sky and transforming it into a multi-coloured dome.

At first almost inaudible, a tiny twitter came from the nearby wooded fort. And then, very slowly, this first note was followed by another and then another. An unseen feathered orchestra was preparing for a dawn recital. Radiant light poured down over the mountains, changing the fields into pools of gold. And gradually the whole symphony of bird song spread through the groves of trees around the house. The surrounding landscape was alive with light and the dawn chorus was heralding in the arrival of the new day.

That dawn was many years ago but it had opened a door into an awareness of the beauty of the coming of a new day. Years afterwards, I remembered it as I watched another new dawn as the sun rose over the Sea of Galilee. I felt that heaven was reaching down and blessing the earth. And now, I had my third experience as I strolled slowly around the garden intrigued by the sparkling early-morning cobwebs. Shrubs were shrouded in shimmering veils. What an amazing complexity of designs the spiders could create in one night. And the whole garden was full of fresh smells that seeped into my senses. A wave of tranquility washed over me, forming a peaceful inner pool. This pool would remain calm no matter what chaos the day might bring.

Inner Sanctum

Let me steal five minutes
To welcome in the dawn,
To touch its dewy fingers
As they creep across the lawn,
To watch beneath a misty tree
The sun roll back the night,
Its beams transforming darkness
With soft translucent light,
To hear the birds awaken
With delight to meet their day
Let their happiness infuse me
To meet my day their way;
Let this tranquil scene give balance
To the busy day ahead,
To create a tranquil pool
For withdrawal inside my head.

Crash Me Not into a New Day

Let me unfold gently
Into a new day
As the sun calmly
Edges above the horizon
Before blazing into a new dawn;
As the birds softly
Welcome the light
Before bursting into
The full dawn chorus;
As the cow rising
stretches into
Her own body
Before bellowing
To her companions.

May I, too, slowly absorb
Be calmed and centred
By the unfolding depths
Of this new day,
So that my inner being
Will dance in harmony
With whatever
It may bring.

Repairs and Maintenance

Showers have totally taken over from baths. Far quicker. Far more hygienic. They better suit our modern world. Who has time in today's world to take a bath? Even the very word 'take' a bath conjures up images of taking something from a former time that does not quite belong in today's world. You are not quite with it. Neither are you entitled to 'have' a bath. This implies that you are wasting time having something you could well do without. It is a waste of time. You waste time waiting for the bath to fill, and then more time getting the water to the right temperature to make sure that you will not be frozen to death or roasted alive ... This all takes time. Time that you really do not have. And after all that, do you actually come out of a bath well washed? From a hygiene point of view a shower is far more efficient. The polluted water disappears instantly down the plughole rather than swirling around your cleansed body in a foamy sludge.

So, all in all, a bath is a sheer waste of time. Let's get rid of all baths once and for all!

But hold on a minute! Before we throw the bath out with the bath water, let's think it out again. Let's look at having a bath – or taking a bath – from a different perspective. Having a bath is about more than washing the dirt away. A shower does that more than adequately, but a bath does far more. A shower cleans the body, but a bath cleans the body and the mind. A shower is about getting it done, while a bath is about enjoying the experience. While a shower is a necessity, a bath is a luxurious experience. And life is really not about getting to where we are going but about enjoying the journey. A bath captures this perfectly; it is all about the journey. Enjoying the now!

To begin, you pin a notice on the bathroom door: 'Please do not disturb.' Do not turn on the ceiling light; you cannot relax with a light beaming down on top of you – you might as well be on the table in an operating theatre. So keep away from the light switch. Then you gather up your best bath oils and as the tap water begins to flow you pour in the essences. Be generous. This is no time for economy! Collect all your scented candles, preferably lavender-scented. Lavender is the queen of relaxation, but you may like to intertwine it with rose petals or jasmine. Whatever you fancy does you good. This is all about *doing you good*. Pack your worries into a black bag and park it outside the locked door. Place a scented cushion at the end of the bath to rest your head. Place your candles all along the bath edge, leaving an entry space for you. Then light up. When the bath is foaming and the room is glowing, you slide blissfully in and rest your head on the scented cushion. Then wait for wonders to happen!

Rejuvenation

Swirls of steam shroud the body
Of an old, old woman.
I crawl feebly over the bath edge
And submerge into the sudsy warmth.
My children are parasites
My husband unloving
My friends demanding;
I want to die.
My body dissolves
My mind evaporates
I become nothing,
Drifting into oblivion.
A few hot-water top-ups
And an hour later
I come back together.
My children are independent,

My husband adoring
My friends supportive.
It's good to be alive,
And I high-step
Out of the bath
Vibrant and beautiful
And the old lady
With all her problems
Disappears down
The plughole.

Afternoon Tea

The very term 'afternoon tea' conjures up images of genteel ladies in regency elegance sipping tea from bone-china cups in gilded drawing rooms or under spreading trees on immaculately trimmed, sweeping lawns. The practice probably commenced in those great houses where leisure seemed to be a way of life and eating a nonstop event, at least for those living upstairs. On recently viewing *Lords and Ladles* on television, I was amazed at the amount of food that was consumed in one dinner sitting alone. But while other meals were accompanied by a certain amount of ritual and formality, afternoon tea had about it an air of leisure and relaxation. It was a time to unlace the rigid corsets and loosen up, to play with the released nursery-bound children or to enjoy croquet on the lawn.

And in the humbler homes of the people who actually worked the land, afternoon tea – with a different title and in different surroundings – also took place. In my childhood it was known as the 'four o'clock tea'. It provided a welcome rest during long afternoons of hard work. It was probably introduced to break the long fast between dinner and supper, from 1pm to 7pm. In those days dinner was the main meal of the day on the farm and was always served at one o'clock; supper was served when the cows had been milked, at seven o'clock. That was a long, hungry span for workers and hence the practical need for the four o'clock tea.

During the summer months of hay-making this tea was brought out into the fields and became known as 'tea in the meadow'. As well as the basic brown bread, there was usually a homemade apple cake or some other treat. So even on a working farm, that tea also had connotations of leisure and little extras. While having 'tea in the meadow', there was time for a chat, lying on the warm hay, chewing a sop of hay and watching the beautiful butterflies waft around. Time for the children, who were part of the workforce, to explore the surrounding dykes and ditches for frogspawn and birds' nests. So in whatever location they took place, these teas had about them a sense of taking life a bit easier.

Thankfully, the tradition of afternoon tea has survived and in recent times has made a big comeback. One of the hallmarks of afternoon tea is that location is all-important. In pleasant surroundings, with the

right ambience, good food and enjoyable company, these occasions can be delightful. Some hotels now make it one of their priorities. Maybe in our hurried world we have become aware of the need to enjoy the relaxation that is associated with afternoon tea. Nobody goes out to have afternoon tea in a hurry. It is all about taking time and enjoying the now.

An Ordinary Day

I t was just an ordinary day. Sometimes it is only in
retrospect you realise that an ordinary day was not
as ordinary as it seemed at the time. It could well be
an occasion that might never happen again.

A few years ago an afternoon tea that friends and I
shared was one of those days. At the time we thought
that it was simply a lovely experience that we would
all enjoy again. We were unaware that it was a once-
off and that we would never again have that time
together.

Norma and Brian had cleared a space in the depths
of nearby Drumkeen Wood and had built an wonderful house there, surrounded by trees that blended
into the wooded background. To reach the house you
made your way up a curving tree- and fern-lined
rugged lane, and after rounding many curves you
came to the tree-encircled house, totally at one with
its surroundings.

Woodturner Brian had carefully preserved the trees
that had had to be removed for the building and they

were stacked up in a garden shed. Later he created beautifully crafted tables and lamps. I have one of those lamps and it is a joy to run my hand over the smooth surface of the wood.

The house was perfect for Norma. In a raised area all around it, she nurtured her wild-flower gardens. She loved butterflies – and she herself was like one of her beautiful butterflies, at home in this natural space between rocks, ferns and wild flowers. She had exquisite taste and graced the house with delicate items of great beauty. A natural conservationist, she constantly litter-picked the roads leading to their laneway and diligently planted trees and wild flowers with the local Tidy Towns group. Being of a charming and gentle disposition, she made many friends and we all loved her.

One sunny summer's afternoon she invited her friends for tea. She had placed a circular table, draped with an embroidered cloth, in the window recess of her front room, looking out over the garden. We gathered around the table, laden with Norma's beautiful delicate china and amazing baking. She was a superb cook and had the art of exquisite presentation. It was a delightful afternoon. Common interests of reading, painting and gardening made for great conversation – which confirms Lady Macbeth's belief:

To feed were best at home;
From thence, the sauce to meat is ceremony;
Meeting were bare without it.

After tea we meandered around the house and garden. On the mantelpiece was an eye-catching greeting card of a lady in a white trailing dress and red hat, relaxing in a white hammock. Annette, who was present with us, had sent it to Norma while on holiday. The card somehow captured the spirit of Norma. I took the card home and later painted the picture for her.

Norma, who was a nurse, had a plan to special-ise as a hospice nurse, and with her kind and gentle disposition she would have brought solace to many. But it was not to be. Soon after that afternoon tea, while she was out with Brian and her friend Helen and Helen's husband, Norma collapsed. She was diag-nosed with a brain tumour. Once recovered from the initial shock, Annette suggested: 'Let's make the time left for Norma as enjoyable for her as possible. At least she has *now*.' And Annette was not indulging in wish-ful thinking; she made it happen.

And so we had lovely days out all around West Cork. We would get so engrossed in conversation we often went astray. On one of those days, driv-ing to Gougane Barra, Annette announced, 'I think

the turn-off we should have taken is about four miles back!' And indeed it was.

Norma loved every moment of those precious days. And when the time came, she was cared for by Helen and wonderful hospice nurses in her own home, where she died surrounded by those she loved.

Enshrined in my mind is a golden cameo of that special afternoon in the wood when we had so enjoyed Norma's wonderful afternoon tea. And we had all thought that it was just an ordinary day. It was a great reminder to me: cherish the moment as it may never happen again.

Finding My Feet

The voice of the man guiding the meditation is easy and gentle on the ear. His words waft into our minds like butterflies landing on thistle-down. I am on a weekend meditation retreat in the Dzogchen Beara Buddhist Centre in the depths of West Cork. Time off the treadmill of everyday life.

We came late last night when the mountain was shrouded in darkness and the sea sighing quietly around it. The centre clings to the side of the mountain and you make your way up and down steep paths to the different levels. In the Shrine Room, where the directed retreat is taking place, silence reigns but for the voices of Andrew and Stephanie, who take it in turn to direct the meditation.

Now Andrew is talking about walking meditation. I have often wondered about this. He tells us that as you walk you feel, hear, see and be where you are and that you do it slowly and mindfully. In other words: be there. Into my head swims the words of a song I had long forgotten: 'Slow down, you move too fast'.

Then Andrew suggests that we go out and walk wherever our fancy takes us along the mountainside. It is January, so the paths are muddy with occasional pools of water. I plod along in my well-insulated boots and hear the mud squelch beneath me. It is a satisfying, earthy sound. When it feels as if I might get stuck in the mud I move on to the verge where the grass sinks beneath me and muddy water oozes up between the clumps of weeds. It slushes up around my boots. I wish then that I was barefoot.

Back on the home farm when I was a child we often jumped barefoot into muddy gaps. It was lovely to feel the mud ooze up between our toes. We also jumped into soft, warm cow dung – this was one of the delights of summer days. I know that this may sound slightly disgusting, but as children we delighted in the feel of it beneath our feet. The fields were strewn with cow dung and to land into one with bare feet was sheer sensuous delight. If freshly created, it was like soft green cream that oozed up between our toes forming a kind of poultice for our soles and heels. It was a great feeling – and probably very good for our feet. Afterwards, we would run barefoot through dewy grass and feel the dew course down in warm streams along our legs. We loved it. Who knows but maybe it was from this contact with the earth that our modern body massage

evolved? When I go for reflexology now I wonder if it could all have begun with warm cow dung? In today's world, mud, cow dung and dew are replaced by sweet-smelling oils. But it is all about soothing the senses, whatever balm you use.

Suddenly a curious robin brings me back to the present here in Dzogchen Beara as he comes to investigate. He hops on to a stony ditch beside me and cocks his heads inquiringly. He has no fear of humans. This is his place and nobody has ever done anything to alarm him.

I plod on and wind my way to a donkey sanctuary at the far end of the mountain where deeper mud puts a stop to my gallop. I look down over the mountain, which is wearing a muted winter coat, and the sea below is grey and solemn. It is winter and nature has gone to ground. The scene soothes the mind into a wonderful stillness.

Cow Dung

As a child my feet felt
The three stages of cow dung:
First, warm green slop oozed up
Between pressing toes,
Poulticed sinking heels.
Later sap fermented
Beneath a black crust,
Resisted a probing toe.
Then hard grey patch,
Dehydrated and rough
Beneath tender soles,
Its moisture absorbed
Into growing fields.
Noble cow dung fed the earth
Which gave us our daily bread.

The Wonder
of Wood

This summer I received an unexpected gift, an invitation to visit the studio of wood sculptor Joseph Walsh, a genius who has transformed the art of furniture creation into miracle-making. What had he dreamed up, I wondered? What had he created this time?

His work is inspirational. To stand in the Joseph Walsh studio is to be constantly mesmerised by the startling vision of this extraordinary man. Inspired from an early age by the possibilities of his own creativity, he danced to the music of his own soul. As I stood there now, his imaginative, mind-startling pieces once again held me speechless.

But for me one creation stood out from all the others – a long banqueting table. The pale grey, gleaming surface of this table came alive beneath my gaze. It drove my imagination into high gear. I could almost believe that this tabletop had been moulded in the

depths of the ocean by the tossing to and fro of end-less tides. All along it, waves seemed to roll away in front of you and out of them rose a sea goddess with streaming hair treading the waves. Or so it seemed to me. My mind was set alight. Imagined pictures were flowing across the surface of this table as I gazed at it.

Beneath the tabletop, beautifully moulded, rolling waves of finely crafted wood held this maritime mag-nificence afloat. The entire creation appeared to me to have risen from the depths of the seas, but it had, of course, risen from the depths of the genius of its creator. From conception to completion, this inspired creation was a sheer wave of genius. You had to be overawed by its magnificence.

Out in the workshop a swanlike, elegant master-piece was being created. Destined to bring future viewers into the raised realms of awesome wonder.

Then we went out to an old farmhouse where gen-erations of the Walsh family once lived. Here pieces by the young Joseph sit comfortably amongst the old farmhouse furniture of his ancestors. Was it from such as these that his genius sprang? Was it by these simple pieces that his creativity was nurtured? This creativity that is now flowing around the world into the most exclusive showrooms.

In the grove around the house young trees are thriving, growing in the rich soil of the land. This rich

land that nurtures and supports nature also nurtures the creativity of our inner being.

Coming face-to-face with the creativity of a fellow human raises us to a new level, gifting us with a momentary glimpse of the divine. Another visionary craftsman, William Blake, sensed this when he said, 'Imagination is Evidence of the Divine.' Divinity and creativity are the dance of life, swirling us humans out of the mundane onto an inspirational realm. Endowing us with elusive butterfly wings that float us upwards out of the ordinary into moments of wonder.

Take Good Care
of Me

I am a killer! Give me a house plant and it is dead within a month. My past life is strewn with victims of thirst, light deprivation and malnutrition. This is difficult to understand because I would stay up at night to keep the slugs off my hostas and I almost breastfeed my window boxes to keep them happy, but give me a house plant and all these caring instincts are no more. Overnight I change from a carer into an exterminator. It simply does not make botanical sense. Is there a touch of Dr Jekyll and Mr Hyde here?

But all that could be about to change. Recently my friend Annette brought a gardening friend to visit. She had flown into Cork airport and Annette was driving her to her destination, and *en route* they called in for a walk around my garden. It was January, so the garden was not a thing of great beauty, but fellow gardeners understand, and anyway gardeners never tire of walking around other people's gardens no matter what the season. And, though I am loth to admit it, gardeners also never tire of showing off their gardens. We are probably all exhibitionists at heart.

When Annette arrived she breathed a sense of well-being and vitality. Dressed in a classy black hat, matching coat and high black boots, she was a model for the catwalk. And in her arms she carried a plant that matched the ensemble. Glossy dark green leaves laced with delicate white and rose-tinted heart-shaped flowers. This plant was a statement!

When Annette and her friend had departed, my new plant and I sized each other up. Like any good host, I helped her out of her cellophane travelling coat and she then stood tall and elegant in her full glory. In the equestrian world, experts judge horses by bone structure and lineage. This lady came from a top-class stable. She exuded good breeding. As she was still in her walking shoes, I needed to provide something more suitable. There are times when it pays to be a hoarder and out in my back porch I have a range of pots. Amongst them was a tall, black, imperious-looking model. Perfect! Not for this new arrival a flowery, girly container. She would reject it. So she stepped into this ebony-black pot, which was just right.

You are beautiful, I told her, but you are probably a high-maintenance lady. She looked me straight in the eye and issued an imperious command: You'd

better take good care of me. Once those social pleas-
antries were exchanged I read her calling card. She
was Anthamalia Elegance. The name said it all. Then
I studied her caring instructions. I have a friend who
works in a hardware store and says that most people
do the job first and then read the instructions. I am
one of them. But not on this occasion. I was taking no
chances. A whole new me was emerging. But who-
ever designed her calling card presumed that the host
would know how to interpret the most extraordinary
sign language or else know exactly what to do with
this lady. So it was on to Google.

What did we do before Google brought enlight-
enment into all our ignorant minds? Now, Google,
as you know, don't do things in half-measure. There
was an hour's reading on how to care for my elegant
friend, but the bones of it were that she was an Anthamalia and she came from warm climes; she liked heat
and moisture, but not too much. And the cold was a
no-no. In other words, neither hot nor cold would
please her! She needed good light, but not direct sunlight, so required a veil between her and hot sun. She
required drink, but in measured amounts, so she was
not a roaring alcoholic, but neither was she a teeto-
taler. Having digested all of these instructions, I realised that location was of paramount importance. Then
on further reading I discovered that my guest was a

royal – Princess Amelia Elegance. Wow! This guest had royal requirements.

The most pressing decision was a suitable location to accommodate all her needs. But the first priority, as far as I was concerned, was the need for her to be right under my eye where she would not be forgotten – and, more importantly still, where I could enjoy her. Princess Amelia Elegance and I waltzed around the house trying to decide on the perfect resting place.

Temperature-wise, the kitchen was probably best, but in there the window sill was too high and would not show her off to advantage. And I sensed that she would not approve of that location. She had about her an aura of grandeur, and, furthermore, royals do not quite belong in kitchen quarters. More of a drawing-room model. But, in coming to me, she had come down in the world, so she would have to compromise. The bathroom, except when in use, has sub-zero temperature, so that was out. The hall was too draughty. Another few options did not quite hit the spot.

So eventually we came to the conclusion that the window sill of the front room, which is the runway from the front door to the kitchen, was the best place. There she would be constantly under my eye and would not be forgotten. This window faced southeast, so she would have good light, but the lace curtain would veil her from hot sunlight. In winter, when closing the main curtains at night, I could move her onto a nearby table to avoid the outside chill. She was beside the kitchen, so watering was convenient. And, still more important, she was at the right level to display her dark finery which was set off by the bright light of the window behind her, and this also highlighted her profusion of rose-tinted flowers. Perfect location! We were both happy!

But I was not prepared for the difference that she made to the room. She brought it alive. Every night she waltzes off the window sill and rests on a corner table where her white flowers shine in the soft light of the room. Each morning she steps back up on the window sill to stretch out her elegant leaves against the background light. All day she fills the place with her presence. She has brought a new energy to the room. I am determined that she will not die in my care. Forefront in my mind is her command on arrival: Take good care of me.

I certainly will do my best. But my history is against me ...

PART 2
Roots

My mother and father went out
together to bless their fields.

Beauty from Boredom

The seeds of some precious moments are planted in childhood and in later life are shot into full bloom again by special occasions. As in wild-flower meadows, seeds may remain dormant in our minds for years until the right conditions present themselves and then they spring into life. Such moments are golden. Like dry sponges, children absorb their surroundings.

My daughter takes great delight in reminding me that when she complained as a child that she was bored I told her that only boring people were ever bored! When children are bored they then excavate their inner resources – and inside in each of us is a hidden treasury that we might never quarry but for a little boredom.

I made that discovery many years ago as a child on a sunny evening in Ballybunion. Every evening my mother dragged me to the church while she said her

rosary. After a long, sunny day paddling in the warm
pools between the high rocks and chasing along the
beach, the silence of the shadowy church was unwel-
come. It was simply an intrusion between the glorious
daytime activity and a night at the 'merries', where
rides in the bumpers competed with the one-arm
bandits. Praying in a quiet church was not high on my
list of priorities. My mother was of the 'we shall not
be moved brigade'. She ignored all my manoeuvres
of restlessness and bored sighs and continued praying her rosary silently. I checked the progress of her
fingers along the decades and discovered that she was
not even half-way through the Joyful mysteries – and
that Jesus had yet to be born and then he had to be
presented and lost in the Temple. I was familiar with
his journey from the nightly rosary at home when
my mother told the story of each decade before com-
mencing on the ten Hail Marys. Here she was confined to silent prayer, but this unfortunately removed
the deadline which at home my father provided, much
to our relief. Here there was no one to put a stop to
my mother's religious gallop. So I knew that after the
rosary there would be all the 'trimmings', prayers that
could go on forever. I was supposed to stay kneeling
beside her, but finally, in desperation, after whispering
loudly, 'I'll wait outside', I headed for the back door
of the church.

Outside I sat on a stone wall and viewed the field right across the road. There was not much to view. The field was buried in a wilderness of weeds, briars and bushes. But as I sat there swinging my legs in boredom, my eye fell on a beautiful red poppy. It made me sit up and take notice. I was amazed to see it. Where had it come from? Had it been there last night? If it was, I had not seen it. But now it got my undivided attention. It was incredibly tall, elegant and delicate, and the most gorgeous shade of deep rose red. It was mesmerising. It moved gently in the breeze like a ballerina and I almost expected it to rise up out of the ground and float across the field to me. I was still gazing at it in rapture when my mother came out of the church.

That was a precious moment born out of sheer boredom that created in me a keen awareness of magic moments.

A Memory

The waste ground was choked with weeds
That grew above her head
But in the middle of this bloomed
One flower of golden red.

The little child came every day
To gaze upon the scene
The flower it was the loveliest sight
That she had ever seen.

This flower took root and blossomed
It grew inside her head
And led her on to lovely things
Long after it was dead.

That poppy never faded.

The Gap

Aploughed field is the beginning of a story to be told. It is a blank canvas waiting for the full picture to be filled in. Whenever I see a ploughed field I feel a sense of wonder at the miracle that is nature. Over the years, farming methods have changed enormously, but we still plough the fields and depend on God or nature or whatever you believe in to continue the story. We still do winter ploughing, turning up the brown sods so that the natural winter elements will crumble and soften the earth and make it ready to receive the seeds of spring more kindly. It is a miracle in the making.

My love of ploughed fields comes from the days when my mother dispatched me with an enamel jug of warm tea with wedges of her brown bread resting across the top, to feed the ploughman, my father. My mother's motto was – keep the working men out in the fields well fed and nurtured; they care for the earth that gives us our daily bread.

The ferns on the ditch of the boreen up to the

field were brown and drooping, exhausted from the struggle to hold their ground against wind and frost. The sinking sun shot dying rays through their wilting fronds, illuminating them with touches of bronze beauty.

I was alone in a meditative, silent world where nature was resting for the winter. There was a sense of an enclosed cloister between the high mossy ditches on either side of me. It was a time for absorbing, 'poderawling' and dawdling. The crows were sweeping home in black clouds across the sky to settle down for the night on the tall trees in the haggard down by the house.

The stony boreen sloped upwards to the High Field. I watched my step carefully so as not to disturb the tea in the jug and cause it to splash upwards against the bread. Eventually I reached the gap. I stood there and looked west across the field. It was the era of the horse, when things took time. Outlined against the skyline and illuminated by the dying rays of the sinking sun was the horse, the plough and the man. It was a sacred moment of total harmony between animal, man and creation, a little cameo that created an awareness for life of this blessed trinity.

A Ploughed Field

Oh brown ploughed field
What an ancient skill
Is in your turned sod.
A skill inherited
By generations of earthy men.
Beneath the sheltering trees
You cover the hillside
In a cloak of brown velvet
What a softness is yours;
You are an open book
Yet to be written:
The virginity of the upturned sod
Waiting to be fertilised
By the hands of man
And nurtured by the warmth of nature.

The Well

We called it the Fairy Well. Its deep shimmering waters held the secrets of a long-forgotten ancient world about which we knew very little. The roof of the well arched back into the base of the tree-covered hill of our fairy fort. The fort was as much part of us as Nana was, in her comfortable armchair by the open fire. We knew nothing of the origins of the old fort, but heard adults talk of ancient warring tribes and the need for lookout points. But to us the fort was fairyland and its Fairy Well was a magical gateway, a gateway that led deep down into a mysterious world of the unknown.

The well was the source of sparkling buckets of clear spring water that bubbled up unceasingly from the bowels of the earth. But for us children it was also a source of hours of imaginative play in the stream that meandered out around the large moss-covered stone at its entrance. You could kneel on that stone and, holding firmly onto the branches of the over-hanging tree, poke your head in under the soft mossy

arch that curved back into the hill and peer down into the shimmering water that reflected your face in its brown depths. The flat surface of the big stone was kind to bare knees, or to young bottoms if you chose to sit on it and dance your feet in the stream outside. On sunny days the warmth of the stone was welcoming, but in chilly weather it did not invite togetherness. You would not dare put an exploratory toe into the well itself as this was sacred, clear spring water reserved for drinking or for making tea, which was the precious beverage of the household. Nothing but a spotlessly clean white enamel bucket or shining tin gallon was allowed into that well to withdraw the sparkling spring water. Even the cows and horses knew better than to pollute its pristine waters with their slobbering jaws, but this was probably also due to the fact that in the stream outside they had an ample supply of clear water.

The magic of the well was that it never went dry. It was a constant source of giving – the earth gave its goodness to us – always. When you pushed the bucket down into it depths, the water at first resisted you and then gulped into openness and flooded into the bucket, and immediately replacement water gurgled up from the bowels of the earth. It was a pool of plenty. It was magical. The more we drew out of that well the more came forth. Looking back now, I wonder is our pool of human creativity like that old well? Does stimulation induce more creativity?

The hilly fort encompassing that Fairy Well was a series of humpbacked mounds. To preserve its antiquity from agricultural interference, my father, as a young man, had planted trees in the fort, resulting in a sheltered, wooded area carpeted with years of accumulated leaves and fallen branches. It was a haven for wildlife and every morning came alive with the dawn chorus. In spring bluebells sprouted up through its soft brown carpet and turned it into a sea of blue. During summer wild woodbine trailed along its edges and in autumn briars laden with blackberries asked to be picked. In winter it breathed mystery when snow covered it in blankets of white silence.

Going to the Well

She lifts the bucket
Of clear spring water
From the deep brown well.
Before she rests it
On the flat stone outside,
The wells refills
Gurgling up from the
Bowels of the earth
Refreshed by use
Like her own pool
Of creativity.

The Fort Field

Some farm fields took their turns as meadows or tillage fields but the Fort Field was constantly grazed by the cows and horses. This long, sloping field faced south and flowed gently down towards the river valley. This field was a place of many joyful and ecstatic moments.

In it was a deep stream that tumbled down from the glen further up the valley which satisfied all the cows' drinking needs on summer days. After early-morning milking they spread themselves out all over it in a patchwork quilt – shorthorns, friesians, whiteheads and bawneys. Late in the evening, awaiting milking, they gathered in multi-coloured clusters contentedly chewing the cud.

At other times it was the domain of the horses, who, when released from a hard day's work, galloped around, bucking their rumps into the air with the thrill of release from the restraining harness. Then they buried their hot noses in the tumbling water of the cool stream and afterwards rolled down the soft

sloping surface in an exultation of freedom.

In autumn the Fort Field was dotted with white button mushrooms and the trees along the ditches were rich with hazelnuts.

Resting your back against a tree trunk you could look down over the farm fields – some deserted, others full of grazing animals – and catch glimpses in the valley below of the river that meandered along between the ditches and under a small stone bridge into the wood beyond. Across the river the fields rolled away into a purple haze where animals became faraway dots, and finally the fields disappeared into rolling hills that rose into the Kerry Mountains.

In this hilly field you could stretch out on the soft grass and look up at the sky, watching the clouds, and wonder at the synchronisation of birds in flight. They never seemed to lose their flock formation but flew in total harmony of movement.

Close to the Earth

Come to a quiet place,
A place so quiet
You can hear
The grass grow.
Lie on the soft grass,
Run your fingers
Through the softness
Of its petals
And listen;
Listen to the earth,
The life pulse
Of us all.
Rest your body
Against its warmth;
Feel its greatness,
The pulse and throb,
The foundation
Of the world;
Look up into the sky,
The all-embracing sky,
The canopy of heaven.
How small we really are;
Specks in the greatness
But still a part of it all.
We grow from the earth
To find our own place.

The Sacred Earth

There is a certain magic about the first day of May. You feel like dancing out and washing your face in the morning dew. This is the month that finally kicks shut the door of winter and the countryside starts to blossom. The bounty of the earth begins to appear. It is time to bless the earth and give thanks to the Creator for the gifts bestowed on us. To ask for an awareness of our responsibility to creation.

On that day I go out with holy water and bless my garden. It is my small portion of creation for which I am wholly responsible, and I need to take special care of it and invoke blessings to help me to do so. It is a great day to lie down on the grass and look up at the sky and feel at one with creation.

This is what Rogation Days are all about. I always loved the sound of the word 'rogation'. It rolls off the tongue like water dancing over stones. It comes from the Latin verb *rogare*, which means 'to ask'. And Rogation Days are all about asking. The pagans asked the gods to bless their crops and the practice later found

its way into Christianity. In the Christian Church it dates back to the fifth century and the practice found its way from France to Ireland. The chances are, of course, that our own Druids were already practising it here. In one sense, it is all about love of the land and intercession with the creator to take care of it.

It is surely symbolic that Rogation Days are hinged to the celebration of the Ascension, which is usually in late April, with summer on the horizon. All things are rising, growing and blossoming. For the farmers it is a time of growth on which their very livelihood depends. And so, long ago, they blessed the earth, asking the Creator to take care of all things planted. Because I grew up with the Rogation Day tradition I still go out on May Day and bless my garden.

The Rogation Day ritual of blessing the fields was a link between the known to the unknown. We were invoking God to stoop down and bless our place. As a child it would not have surprised me one little bit if the clouds had opened and a hand reached down in blessing. It had a sense of the mystical, the magical and the natural.

On that Sunday morning my mother brought home from Mass a large whiskey bottle full of holy water. On the way home in the horse and cart it gurgled on her lap, and on arrival she placed it on the parlour table, where it stood like a sentry waiting to be called into action. Then she fed the hungry and when all her jobs were done, she and my father went out together to bless their fields.

Behind the house was the field where most of our food was grown – potatoes, cabbage, turnips, rhubarb and all kinds of everything that my mother tried her hand at. She was one of those people who got slips from neighbours, and also bought multiple packets of seeds – and expected them all to grow. And mostly they did.

From here she led the way from field to field and we all trailed after her. My mother was seldom in a hurry and believed that you gave every occasion the required amount of time, and on this particular occasion, which she deemed to be of major importance, she slowed to a snail's pace. This gave us all time to investigate our favourite corners. We went from one field to another, but when we got to the Brake Field where wheat, barley and oats were turning the brown sod to green, there was extra sprinkling of holy water. Because here grew the wheat that would later be milled for flour to make our bread, and oats and barley that would come back from the mill as grain to feed the farm animals.

Then to the Well Field, Carey's Field, the Kiln Field, Páirc na gCapall, Páirc na gCloch, all providing grazing for the animals. Then down through the hilly Fort

Field and along by the old fort where my father had planted trees.

This brought us to the meadows along by the river. The first one was called the Small Meadow and was tucked into a sheltered little corner under the hill where the ditches were strewn with wild woodbine that would later be in full bloom when we were hay-making. The scent of that woodbine was a joy to the senses. Our sense of smell must be one of our most evocative senses and to this day I come to a standstill at the first whiff of wild woodbine; I close my eyes and am back in that little meadow. Then we moved on to the Big Meadow, the Middle Meadow and the Lyne Field along by the river, and then beyond it to a long finger of a field called Méar na hAbhann.

By then my mother had lost some of her entourage who were distracted away in different directions, but some of us stuck with her, including my father, who was not as much into holy water as my mother was. He was also not big into praying, but he believed strongly in the connectedness of the earth with the sacred. His God was mostly out in the fields. He found a deep peace out there in the silence and tranquility of the land. On that day, I think my parents, who had very different outlooks on life, were in total harmony in their awareness of their dependency on the land and their appreciation of the earth that fed us all. They were very conscious of their responsibility in caring for the earth and my father was constantly impressing that on us. His warning of: 'Wrong nature and you pay a terrible price' forever echoes in my mind.

Months later, on the evening of the threshing when all the grain was gathered into the loft over the cow stalls, my parents came together again to survey the fruits of the earth and of their year's labour. They stood silently at the door of the barn and viewed the mounds of golden wheat, barley and oats stretched out in heaps along the floor. It was their harvest thanksgiving and a moment of shared thankfulness.

Walk the Fields

When I go home
I walk the fields,
The quiet fields
Where the warm dew
Had squelched between
My childish toes,
To sit beneath
The cool oak and ash
That sheltered
My adolescent dreams.
These trees stand
With leafy arms
outstretched
Like lovers
Not in passion
But with gentle
Sighs of contentment.
I watch the cows
Graze peacefully
Beside the river
Curving its way
Through furzed inches
Into the woods beyond.

This is a holy place
Where men have worked
Close to God's earth
Under the quiet heavens.

PART 3
Special Moments in the Garden

The garden wrapped me in
its fragrant arms and would
not let me go.

Dancing with
the Day

The beautiful snowdrop brought me to a standstill. So pure, white and delicate that you wondered how it had pushed its fragile head, with all its perfection, up through the cold, hard earth. Not a blemish to be seen on its dainty, drooping, bell-like head. A miracle of nature. It was the first sight of spring in the garden. And I had missed its arrival.

We were after a week of bad weather, ranging from harsh cold to teeming rain, not encouraging work out in the garden. But this day was different. As soon as I woke I sensed the difference. There was a mildness in the air and when I came out the back door with a bucket of waste for the compost bin, I knew the day had a different feel to it.

On my way to the bin I saw the snowdrop, and that stopped me in my tracks. Where there is one snow-drop there are others, and so I dropped my bucket and went in pursuit of miracles. They were hidden in every corner. Shyly tucked away under overhanging shrubs, around the bases of trees and roses, and even up through stony gravel paths. Then I came on a tiny cluster of them trying desperately to make their way out from under two heavy logs. I shifted the logs and could almost hear them sigh with the relief of release.

All around them the hellebores were just beginning to come forth. They too are the hidden ladies of the garden, with soft, round faces hiding under large green hats. I needed to walk around the paths a few times to see them all because if approached from the wrong angle these ladies were completely hidden. So I brought out a pruner to trim back their large green hats in order to give light to their beautiful faces and encourage them to glow and grow.

And all the time the staunch Daphne Jacqueline Postill spread her veil of gorgeous scent all around. The garden wrapped me in its fragrant arms and would not let me go. It was inviting me to have the first dance of the year. So I decided that we would have lunch together. It was mid-January and a bit early in the year for dining outside, but this day was a special gift. So I accepted it with open arms. I sat with my tray in a shady corner under Uncle Jacky's apple tree and as I dined the birds put on an open-air concert. It was good to be alive.

Red and Yellow

Opening the back door I gasped in delight. Every pot and tub in the backyard glowed with gorgeous red tulips and butter-yellow daffodils. Their vibrancy washed over me and filled me with delight. I had been away for a few days - and now this! While I was absent it had all happened. Nature had been at work. The sun had shone and in its warmth out stepped the elegant tulips and golden trumpet daffodils.

It was very early for the tulips, but they had been coaxed out ahead of time. The sun had wooed them into dancing with the daffodils. They filled the heart with warmth and comfort. A smile flooded my face and a thrill of joy poured down my spine. Tulips are so beautiful! They are elegant and vibrant, like classy ladies dressed for a splendid ball. I danced up the backyard and through the garden gate. Here too the waves of red and yellow continued. They washed through the hellebores and shone through the fresh, delicate green leaves of the acers. I waltzed along the paths,

ooh-ing and aah-ing at each corner. It was a constant unfolding of delights. The colour glowing around the garden flowed into my mind and washed it full of warmth. It raised me up.

Last October a sack of these beauties had come from our local West Cork Bulb Centre, which is just up the road from me. Brian, who runs this haven of delight, had landed a bag of bulbs inside my front door and I got planting. It was the first time that I had gone mad with tulip planting. The bulbs were firm, fat and pregnant with future promise. And, boy, had they delivered! What a joy! The following day I breakfasted and lunched out in their midst to truly absorb the beauty that surrounded me. For late March the weather was amazing. A day of warm sunshine. I idled it away listening to the birds and soaking in the glory of the garden.

Black Gold

Come spring, when I need to gee-up my roses and enrich my compost heap, I ring Conor, who has a large stable of horses outside the village and I inquire about the condition of his horse manure. What I need is old, well-rotted manure, not fresh steaming deposits that would scorch my rose roots. For some reason, which I cannot quite explain, I do not use the word 'dung', instead I say 'manure'. Yet I was reared on a farm where we were familiar with the word 'dung', which was in everyday use then.

There was no other way to describe what accumulated over winter outside the stables and stalls. The dung simply piled up during those winter months when the animals were brought in off the fields from the cold and housed in stables and stalls on beds of straw. This provided warmth and comfort for them. To keep them dry and clean, the floors of their houses had to be brushed out daily. So, over winter, large dunghills rose up outside the doors of the outhouses around the farmyard. That's what we called them,

'dunghills', and every spring this dung was drawn out to the fields with a horse and butt, and used to fertilise the land for growing the crops. The word 'dung' was part of our farm vocabulary. But with the change of farming methods the cow dung become 'slurry', and only the horses stood over what they produced. And as part of that transition our terminology got changed to 'manure'. I'm not quite sure when, how or why that came about.

Was it that the word 'dung' was perceived as being a bit coarse and raw, and that 'manure' was more polite and acceptable? Was the word 'dung' somehow damaging to our delicate sensibilities? Had it something to do with the fact that when bags of artificial fertiliser were introduced on to the land that this was somehow perceived as more refined? It was certainly less smelly. But in Jerusalem a few years ago I was surprised to discover that one of the city gates was known as the 'Dung Gate' or 'Gate of Dung'. Nobody batted an eyelid. So how come what is acceptable in Jerusalem is perceived as not quite so at home?

But no matter what we call it, when I make my annual visit to Conor's stables and see a mountain of black horse dung, I dance with delight. I climb over the freshly piled mounds at the front to reach the old, well-rotted black squelchy stuff at the back. Back there lies the real deal! It opens up like layers of rich dark fruitcake when your ease a spade down into it. Fat, happy worms glide between the layers. It would gladden the heart of any gardener. I glow with delight! Then I know how a prospector feels when he discovers pure gold nuggets. One day I was so thrilled that I danced with delight on top of a black dunghill up at the riding stables.

Ted, an Englishman who is the horse whisperer of the stables, thinks that my reaction to horse dung is hilarious. He helps to shovel it into bags and we bring it back to my garden and mix it up with my own homemade compost. Then I stand back and glow with satisfaction at the sight of this huge compost heap full of worms and future promise. One evening after one such day, Ted met my daughter and told her with great amusement, 'I never saw anybody to get as excited about horse shit as your mother.'

So maybe it does not really matter what we call it! It is simply Black Gold.

Blue Brilliance

Yesterday the grove at the top of the garden was a green oasis. This morning it is awash with blue. The bluebells have arrived, a tumbling cascade of blue confusion massed amongst green waves, spilling their wild scent all over the grove. They slide down over the stone ditch into the garden and cheekily shoulder up between the imperious tulips. This is *their* place! Not drafted in from foreign parts like the royal tulips looking down on them! These are no soft, powder-blue genteel ladies of the court, but brash blue cheeky street urchins, weathered old men of the soil and wild women who have sprung from the bowels of the earth. They are tough old natives. Seasoned campaigners with a strong sense of belonging. Every year they arrive unannounced and every year they push the boundaries of their domain outwards. They want more land. We wage a constant guerrilla warfare. They shoot up from unexpected corners where they have no right to be. But when I try to contain them they shoot defiantly from behind another shrub or tree.

They are the guerrilla warriors of the garden. And they shall not be moved. They are indomitable. By the laws of nature they belong out in the woods and wild places, but they abide by no laws. They were here before me and they will be here after me. To them I am a blow-in. When I am gone they will encompass the whole place in a cloak of blue. They shall overcome!

In an ancient fort beside my childhood home they covered the tree-shaded historic mounds and hollows in waves of blue profusion. Here they had a blue republic with no one to curb their rampant boundary-bashing. We ran through them and rolled down the mounds over them and picked huge bunches of them, filling jampots around the house with their scented blue brilliance. They were the makers of memories.

Each year they arrive early in my sheltered garden and within weeks will cover nearby Drumkeen Wood in a sea of blue waves. They pour down the wood slopes and fill our senses with delight.

We pick them, smell them, enjoy them. Their profusion is glorious!

Fresh Flowers

Give me a bunch
Of dew-fresh flowers
What if they will not last?
I cannot live in the future,
The present is all I ask.

Is there anything more delightful than an unexpected bunch of fresh flowers? They set your heart aglow. Not the cellophane-wrapped flowers on your birthday or Mother's Day – and they are great too – but a bunch that comes totally out of the blue. They sweep in the door in a blaze of colour and light up your day. You receive them with open arms. If they are flowers from someone's own garden, you are receiving a double-decker gift. Because not only are you receiving their flowers, but also the gardener's dedication, work, love and time. Still smelling of the earth and the warmth of the sun, these flowers bring the soul of their garden to you.

These fresh beauties need instant sustenance to keep them glowing, so straight into a bucket of water they go. This gives you time to entertain your generous benefactor while the flowers drink deeply in the bucket. Anyone bringing such a gift deserves a warm welcome and the best welcome of all is time for tea and talk.

After your guest has gone, you slowly savour your flowers and give them all the attention they deserve. You inhale their essence and enjoy their touch and freshness. They soak into your senses and lift your spirits. Next you must decide where to put them: location − location − location! Your head tells you a cool room or the still cooler hallway is best. But in there they will not be constantly under your eye. They will be wasting some of their 'sweetness on the desert air'. On the kitchen table they will give you non-stop joy. They may not last as long here but while they last they will give many moments of delight. When you come into the kitchen in the morning they will have filled it overnight with their heavenly scent and the very sight of them will kickstart your day in the right direction. And throughout the day they will stimulate your happy hormones. So, the kitchen table it is!

Then for the container. Long-stemmed flower-shop classy ladies demand crystal cut-glass vases to better display their elegant legs. But the more sensuous earthy garden flowers belong in a jug. There is nothing pretentious about either of them – a solid crockery jug and garden flowers simply look good together. So after a quick poke around at the back of the kitchen press out comes a fine big open-mouthed old jug ready to grace any occasion. Mellowed and colour-muted from wear, she makes no attempt to outshine her colourful cargo. The flowers shuffle around in her spacious surroundings until they are all comfortable and then they lean out over the sides and survey their surroundings. They will give days of delight.

But if your gardening friends are not falling in the door to you with homegrown bouquets, you can always cut your own, assuming, of course, that you have your own to cut. If not, you are missing out on one of life's joys. Gardening ladies who know such things – and who am I to question their expertise – say that morning is the best time to cut your flowers. And what a delightful way to begin any day. It is uplifting to traipse around the garden in the early morning, drifting from one cluster of beautiful blooms to the next, deciding which might dance best together. You are mixing the colours for a masterpiece in the making. The finished picture will look best if your colour choice is finely blended.

Some flowers, like some people, are not happy together and it shows on their faces. Take, for example, the sweet pea. This beautifully scented fragile lady is one of the 'leave me alone' variety. Put her into a vase with any other flower and her beauty diminishes. She prefers her own space. And she is right! Out in the garden, as well as being a thing of delicate beauty, she fills the air around her with the most gorgeous scent. She brings the same scent and beauty indoors. She's an amazing performer, so why would you not comply with her every whim?

The thorny rose is happy to share her vase with anyone, but she is a prickly lady who likes to be in charge. No back row for this bossy lady! She has to be centre-vase. The hydrangea is a floppy, overweight dame who will shove herself in anywhere and you either love her or despise her. She has no pretentions of grandeur and probably looks best in the garden where she can comfortably overflow all around her and fall on top of everyone else. Tulips, unless you are skilled at flower arranging, are best left to reign in their own kingdom outdoors too, and the pretty little snowdrop is so shy and delicate that it feels like slaughter of the innocent to touch her.

But the daffodil is the girl for all occasions. She thrusts her bright, brazen-yellow head up through frozen ground and shouts that it is time to get out of the winter beds and get cracking into spring. She is exactly the stimulant needed to shake the winter cobwebs out of our brains. She will grow anywhere – in a tub, in a window box, under a tree, on the side of a ditch, so if you do not have a garden this girl is happy to be with you wherever you are. Life would be dull without her. And she is great for cutting; definitely the girl for the centre of the kitchen table where she will glow and be a cheerleader for your spirit as it recovers from winter blues. Bring her in and see a smile light up the face of everyone who comes in the door. She looks good in all containers – vases, jars, jugs – on her own or with greenery, and even the slightly regal tulip will be happy to share a bed with her. The daffodil is full of the joy of now.

Sweet Pea

Rain soaked
Summer morning
Tears glistening
On pale pink faces
Of delicate sweet peas.
Easing back their
Curling tendrils
I carefully snip
Their fragile stems.

They arrange themselves
In an old jug
On the kitchen table
Draping over the rim
In multicoloured profusion
Filling the kitchen with
Their exquisite fragrance.

Waiting ...

The bishop is late. That should not surprise me. The bishop is always late. He waits for a full house before making his appearance. A head turner, he loves to be admired, to strut his stuff in front of an audience. He likes centre-stage. Just now it might be annoying him that he is not in the front row but far back in the line of performers. The bishop could well be sulking because more obliging dahlias have come out ahead of him and stolen the limelight.

But he has only himself to blame! It gets tiresome waiting for his grand debut. He dallies and dallies until all the performers are on the stage and then bursts forth with royal aplomb. But all this waiting can be very wearisome. While around him other dahlias come forth, roses bloom and sweet peas fill the air with their fragrance, the bishop in the back row stands brooding in his dark moody robes. And it is my job to keep a watchful eye on sullen slugs brazen enough to attempt to damage his finery. Does he appreciate my efforts? Not the tiniest bit, as it is

all part to his royal requirements.

But the main bearer of the bishop's capricious ways is the solid black iron pot which holds him. This is his throne. His Lordship may be annoyed that it is a simple black pot. With a name like the Bishop of Llandaff, his ancestors probably resided in palaces of grand episcopal elegance. In their time these gentlemen did not come from humble mountain cabins.

But my high and mighty bishop probably does not appreciate the fact that this is no ordinary black pot from whose depths he presides. It is a solid iron model with a history as long-rooted and interesting as his own. This pot has made its way down through generations of hardy potato-picking mountainy farmers. So has its own story to tell. For centuries it fed the tillers of the earth and held their tears during hungry days when they had no potatoes to boil. It came back into action when the green stalks bloomed again. So my little pot has a history as ancient and rich as his grace. But while his lordship strode the corridors of power, this little black pot fed the multitudes who kept the crowns on those royal heads and food in their ample bellies. And ne'er the twain did meet.

But now, here in my backyard, the bishop is dependent on my little black pot to provide him with sustenance. This pot, like its ancestors, is sturdy and reliable and will keep this bishop fed and watered until he eventually decides to blossom. His flowing, dark rich finery is deep-coloured, dull and understated. This sobriety will be a better contrast with his brilliant blooms when they finally decide to come forth. In the meantime they are restrained in bulging buds, arched overhead, and bursting with promise.

And so my little black pot and I wait patiently for his grace to come forth. Early each morning I check and still the bishop holds back.

And then one morning it happened! He came forth with the dawn! And now, behind the rows of roses and sweet peas, towers His Grace. His bulging buds have burst open and emerged from the palace door wearing a rich royal red crown. He is magnificent. A showstopper. Glorious beyond all expectations. He glistens, glows and demands: 'Look at me! Look at me!' I do just that and life lights up. He was worth waiting for. The bishop has taught me that some things will happen only when the time is right.

The Plantsman

The writing on the envelope told who had sent the letter. The address was in beautiful calligraphy and only one friend can write like that. To look at her writing is a pleasure in itself. The envelope was quite bulky so I wondered about its contents. I sat down in a comfortable armchair and donned my glasses. I felt that a moment to be savoured was about to unfold. As usual, her card was a 'wow' one. Don't you love people who take time to select gorgeous cards! They bring joy in the post.

But it was the little cards within the large card that proved more fascinating. On the little card was a poem written by a mutual friend, Barry, who had died months earlier. She had included a poem card for me and another one for anyone I thought worthy of it. Barry was a once-off creation and his wonderful garden centre was an extension of himself. His little poem, like himself and his garden centre, was a blessing.

Hidden behind rows of trees his garden centre

was a secret treasury of wonder. You had to search around West Cork corners to find it, but once discovered you were drawn back like a bee to a honey pot. It personified the sensible advice that the good businessman gave his son: 'Son, if you want to sell, go where the people are; but if you have what the people want, the people will beat a path to your door.' Many of us beat a path to Barry's gate. A lifetime of knowledge and expertise was behind that gate. The limited parking space was edged by a steel creation laden with bird feeders, so that on arrival you were greeted by flights of birds, and in summer a bevy of hanging baskets.

Then you walked along on level ground between rows of healthy rose bushes and perennial plants, then gently climbed upwards until finally you were on a hilltop edged by giant Olearia trees. On your journey upwards you could curve off in many directions to discover surprising hidden corners. But probably the greatest treasure of all was his selection of trees, all carefully labeled to guide the less well-informed – and Barry was always on hand to advise and guide on the wisdom of choice. He loved his trees and undoubtedly over the years contributed greatly to the wise planting and preservation of trees all over West Cork.

As he grew older and frailer he still walked with

his beloved little dog around his garden centre and gently guided and advised. The day that he died I walked around my own garden and thanked him for all the blessings with which he had enriched my life.

A Blessing

May you never be afraid of growing old.
Count the seasons, not the years.

May each of the four seasons bring you something new, wonderful and beautiful.

May the gentle and serene song of the robin in the dull days of winter fill you with joy as you realise he sings in anticipation of the coming spring.

May the wondrous notes of the blackbird in the hush of the summer's evening fill your heart with songs of praise to Him who gives such pleasures in His creation.

May you never feel you have lost your way as you travel the circle of life. For as sure as the leaves fall in autumn and winter, buds are already form-ing for yet another spring. So when you are old

in years, already you are putting on the blooms of
eternal youth to live forever with Him who said,
'I am the Way, the Truth and the Life.'

Composed by Barry G. Shanahan (1929-2017)

In fond remembrance of a saintly soul who walked
amongst us and guided our planting.

An Old Tree

She is my refuge, my restorer … my friend. She can absorb my many moods and meet many needs. She is a companion through the year, through all seasons. She is truly the star performer in the garden.

In May she bursts into gorgeous pink apple blossom. A joy to behold! She brings to mind the first film that I ever saw, *Maytime*, starring Jeanette MacDonald and Nelson Eddie. That was a long time ago. But her roots stretch back to long, long before that time. She is really the grand old dame of the garden, and she knows how to put on a show. But she is not all about show. Within her pink blossoms are the seeds of her future crop of apples. She is about to set out on her annual voyage of apple production and she begins with a flourish.

During the winter months she rests quietly in the centre of the garden not really making her presence felt. Then she is bare-branched, with sections of her ample trunk spreading out in different directions into the earth around her. All garden paths lead to her. Her

dark, gnarled, twisted branches dominate the skyline. With the passage of time, some of her lower branches have cracked and fallen away, leaving short, lichen-covered stubs protruding from her ivied trunk. These are perfect hangers for bird feeders and over winter the birds fly in flurries around her bare base. Against her trunk is an old seat on which many have rested body and mind down through the years. Facing south and surrounded by low-growing shrubs, she provides a sheltered corner in winter and a cool canopy in summer when she has her coat on.

To rest beneath an old tree is a balm for tired minds. Many days I have sought her out when I was in need of physical and mental respite, and she has never failed to come good. Gradually, as you sit with her, she slows you down. Her tranquility spreads into your body and eventually you sit easy. Then, ever so gently, the tranquility seeps into your mind. You become focused on what is all around you, and you are where you are. So often we are not where we are. We are all over the place. Splintered like sawdust with our minds full of chaff. Nature calmly clears that chaff and centres us back within ourselves. A good place to be.

Now it is May and above her quiet, solid base her branches are coming alive. Beautiful pink buds are budding forth from her soft green lichen-covered branches. She is quietly getting ready for the fruiting season ahead. Every year we think that this year it will not happen, but the old tree begins again. She is self-perpetuating. It is an annual miracle. The little apples begin to appear and slowly over the summer months grow bigger and bigger. An occasional one plops to the ground and is welcomed by the birds, wasps and hungry, unidentifiable garden bugs. But the bulk of the apples cling firmly to her arching branches. They shall not be moved!

But, come September, the time to move them has arrived. For the picking of any apple tree, a dry day is best, but when asking this queen to part with her bounty it is vital, as otherwise her enormous branches would drench you with rain. She was planted long before the arrival of the finely nurtured species that will grow to an exact height and width, thus making apple picking a reach-up-from-the-ground job. This grand old lady has never had her tresses trimmed, never been introduced to a curtailing pruner, and so has been free to grow her own way. She is all over the place, reaching for the sky and stretching out over half the garden. Collecting her apples is a test of courage, balance and dexterity. You need to have the climbing skills of a monkey and the long arms of the giant in 'Jack and the Beanstalk'. But there is a man for every job, the only difficulty is to find him! I have a man for all seasons who is capable of doing all things that come his way. And not only can he do it, but he does it with great goodwill and a merry heart.

And so up he crawls along the branches, and on the lower branches he succeeds in getting most of the apples straight into a bucket. But as he goes higher, the job of holding onto the branches requires all his concentration lest he crash-land down into the rose bushes, so we have to settle for shaking the branches. This sends down a cascade of apples. I scramble around hastily to collect these before the next shower makes pulp of those already landed.

You need to keep your wits about you to duck out of the way of earth-bound apples, but it is very invigorating. By lunchtime all the apples have landed, or at least as many as are get-at-able. It is time for lunch, which we decide to enjoy under our now almost denuded tree. It is resting time for body and mind. We survey a job half-done!

Then back to business and we gather up all the apples, filling up rows of boxes with them. They are all sizes and shapes – big, small, bumpy and gnarled, some still sprouting bits of branches. Once boxed, they are borne into the back porch where they are laid out in rows along by the wall. They are a glorious sight and fill the back porch with the unmistakable wild earthy smell of freshly picked apples. The smell permeates into the house, causing callers-in to remark, 'You've picked the apples!' and I ask hopefully, 'Do you want a box?'

The arrival of the boxes of apples into the back porch heralds a day of apple-tart making. These apples, owing to their mode of picking, are not long-lasting. So the time for baking is *now*. The grand old lady of the garden has done her bit. Now it is my turn.

PART 4
Small Kindnesses

You held out a caring hand
When I was full of pain;
You thawed my frozen being
And made me live again.

The Black Bubble

Grief crashed in through the front door, flooded every room and swept out the back door, leaving an all-encompassing sludge of desolation. It paralysed me both mentally and physically. I had not known that bereavement submerged your physical as well as your mental strength. It brought exhaustion with it. It was a huge effort to do anything, a huge effort even to drag myself out of bed in the morning – but to stay there was to be buried under blankets of desolation. The night rekindles the trauma of the experience of loss and in the morning you awaken under waves of despair. A friend who had walked the grief road advised: 'As soon as you wake, get out of bed and straight into the shower. The bed could kill you.' I had no idea if she was right or wrong, but to me this was a frightening foreign zone and she had survived it. She had been there, so she must know what she was talking about. I did as she told me. Then a health guru, who was also a friend, advised that before getting out of the shower you should turn it to cold. A daunting prospect! I yelled with the shock as the freezing water hit me. But it got me moving into the day.

Then the day stretched ahead with no sense or meaning to it. For the funeral you go on auto-pilot and the rituals keep you functioning and moving on. Then it is all over and you are back in the real world. But the real world that you had known is no longer there. You are now living in a black bubble. Outside of it the world that you remember continues to function. But you are not part of it anymore and have no desire to be. How are you to survive without the old structures? You stumble blindly on and grasp at every little aid that eases the pain, even temporarily.

As you journey on you fall into little healing pools. They appear out of the blue and you stumble into them, and they give you temporary respite and the strength to try to keep going on. It could be a chat by a warm fire with a good friend, a walk through a wood, a lovely piece of music, a beautiful flower, a heavenly smell, digging the garden. Kind and understanding friends are the greatest help. Gradually all these comforting experiences begin to weave you back to wholeness. They reach out and encompass you and very slowly you reawaken into a new world. Not the world you once knew, but a different world. And this world has its own beauty. The past is gone

and you remember it with gratitude. But your time is now, and gradually you discover that now is precious.

Kindness

The warmth of your kindness
Kept me in my mind;
Its worth could not be measured
It had goodness undefined.
You held out a caring hand
When I was full of pain;
You thawed my frozen being
And made me live again.

Beautiful Mind

Standing in a tall, slim, elegant vase on the kitchen table a single red rose filled the air with its beautiful smell. The very sight of it warmed my heart and welcomed me home. I knew that Maureen had called because the red rose was her calling card.

Years previously we had both watched Brother Mitchell plant a rose bed in his monastery garden. His roses were all the same rich red and when you stooped to sniff, they enfolded you in their gorgeous deep aroma. Mitch, as we called him, was the bursar at the nearby monastery and kept all their financial affairs in meticulous order.

But when his day's work was done, the other side of Mitch came alive. Then he cast aside all the trappings of work and donned a long, ragged, knitted jumper and an old woolly hat that had long lost its claim to being a fashion accessory. He grasped his wheelbarrow with loving delight and headed for the gardens, where he cracked into action. There he came alive with creativity and enthusiasm.

There he grew all his flowers and produce from seeds, laying them out lovingly in long, precise rows of perfection. In early spring he brought the seedlings forth from his cloches and greenhouse, and spread the results of his labours around the monastery garden. Not given to long-winded conversation, he smiled benignly at you from a distance and kept focused on the job in hand. You felt that you should not stop the flow of his creativity. But should you come on him between jobs, he would lean on his garden spade and engage you in a delightful exchange. After a few moments of chat, a light would go on in your mind and you became aware that this man was connected with his God out here in his garden as much as in the monastery chapel. When you sensed that it was time to move on, you reluctantly said goodbye and walked away feeling that the world was a better place than you had thought.

Some nights when the garden was resting, he joined us at a prayer meeting in the chapel and there he gently eased us on to a higher level of connectedness between God, man and nature. Now that he is gone, his roses are moments of joy and a prayer of remembrance between those of us who knew and loved him.

Uplift

'Fruit of the earth
And work of human hands'
Today I heard
And saw
For the first time
The earth
The human
The divine

Battered Chalice

I t was a silent retreat. There is a lot to be said for a silent retreat, because we all talk too much – I certainly do. Silence is rare and golden. It gives the inner being recovery time and a rest from pouring forth judgemental opinions on all kinds of everything.

The retreat was in the nearby monastery of St Patrick's, Upton, which is a caring centre for adults who cannot cope with the challenges of the outside world. Here they have excellent care in a safe environment, where many of the carers are local and their community is darned into the larger parish community.

One of the residents was Ned, who, due to an unfortunate accident as a child, was brain-damaged and, even though an adult now, still lived in the world of childhood. He had the endearing practice of picking flowers and presenting them smilingly to any adult who came his way.

It was a warm, bright, sunny day in June and the group on retreat left the little chapel and scattered silently around the grounds. I made my way into a

nearby field where I walked along by the ditch, enjoying the sunshine and relaxation. It was good to be alive.

Some of the residents were gathered in a far corner listening to a match on the radio. Cork were playing in a hurling game and when they scored there were shouts of joy, and when groans of disgust came across the field you knew that we were in trouble. Their reaction to the scores reached me in waves of delight and despair, and somehow contributed to the joy of the moment. They were having a great time jumping and yelling and scoring imaginary goals.

Quietly Ned left the group and came across the field picking flowers as he came, and then presented them to me in a little posy. It was a touching moment and I thought: this is an adult behaving like a child. How lovely.

But that evening as we gathered in silence around the altar I perceived things differently. Maybe a day of silence and prayer listening to inspirational talks had opened a door into a more perceptive part of my mind and I saw that Ned, though maybe an adult behaving like a child, was also a host in a battered chalice. I brought the scene home in my head.

Battered Chalice

God's day,
The birds and sun
Celebrate His creation.
Your pick the flowers
With such joy in your hands:
Little child in the body of a man
You are the host in a battered chalice.
'*Duine le Dia*' old people said,
And how wise they were
Because you live within
The circle of God's arm.
Not for you
The snare of this world
You walk above man's narrow vision.

Never Suppress a Good Impulse

A bright, cold frosty morning in February. The phone rang. It was Mary, who lives outside the village. 'Alice, I just want to tell you that your window boxes are absolutely beautiful. We drove past just now they were shining in the sun. They did me good. I thought that I would ring and tell you.'

What an absolutely lovely thing for her to do. It did my heart good that my window boxes brightened up her day, but more so that she took the time to tell me. It made me realise how often we do not bother to voice our appreciative thoughts. How often do we think something like this but do nothing about it? We are too busy to take the time or we think that other people will think it silly, and then all kinds of other thoughts come into our heads. And so we crush the generous impulse and do nothing. That is such a pity.

One of the best pieces of advice that I ever got was: 'Never suppress a good impulse.' Mary had a good

impulse and she went with it, and I benefited from her generosity of spirit. It may be only a little thing in the larger scheme of things, but little things mean a lot. So whenever we get a good impulse, we should go with it, not suppress or over-analyse it. Just do it. Do it *now*! Give somebody the joy of the moment.

Generous impulses come from an unknown source into the creative side of the brain, but if we go into analysis mode the practical side of our brain clocks in and kills the goose that laid the golden egg. Generous people who go with their good impulses make the world a warmer place. You feel better after meeting such people. Others often have the opposite effect. Having met them you feel less well. They make the world a greyer place. And the strange thing is that they are not necessarily people to whom life has dealt a tough hand. They just enjoy spreading misery. These are the wet-day people of the world.

So let's be thankful for the Marys of the world who believe in spreading their joy around.

A Touch of Spring

Spring came today
And walked with me
Up the hill,
Breathing softness in the air,
Opening gates within my head.
The birds felt his presence,
Pouring forth symphonies
Of unrestrained welcome.
It was mid-January
And he just came
To have a peep,
Trailing behind him
Along the valley
Wisps of purple veils.

Let It Be

It was an ugly experience. A tidal wave of raw rage had crashed in my door. The sanctity of my home had been desecrated and my sense of wellbeing breached.

That night sleep evaded and as I watched the grey dawn creep in the window I realised that for this trauma there would be no quick fix. My inner sense of serenity had been eroded. How could I repair what had been damaged? I had no answer.

During the following days the lines of the old Beatles song kept drifting into my mind, and I hoped there would be an answer, and I could perhaps let it be? So I tried to let it be. That was easier said than done! But I had no choice, as I had no solution. So I had to let it be.

But would there be an answer? I had always loved that old song, but had not listened to it for years. Now I found myself listening to it on YouTube and found it strangely comforting. As I listened, I wondered would there be an answer?

Then the answer came. Unexpectedly, out of the blue. It was a phone call from a friend whom I had not seen for several years. He rang to say that he was planning to give a special course and would I be interested. I was!

Years previously this enlightened man had attempted to introduce me to the stillness and the treasury of inner being, but he was casting pearls before swine. At the time I was too immature and self-opinionated to appreciate the richness of his gift. Now I was ready. The mills of God grind slowly but they grind exceedingly well. Maybe the Beatles were right!

So began a healing and enriching journey. This amazing course was food for the mind, soul and body. It revealed truths that gave meaning to much that had been beyond my understanding. I was on an enlightening inner journey where a whole new landscape was revealed. Windows of revelation were gently eased open and into my mind poured healing light. My whole being was cleansed and renewed.

One day, in the middle of the course, I suddenly realised that I was being healed. The ugliness was being eroded, slowly flushed out of my system. The wisdom of ages absorbed during this amazing course was repairing the damage. This *was* the answer!

And so now, in hindsight, I realise that the experience, like so many other ugly happenings in life, though highly undesirable and traumatising at the time, was part of a learning curve. I am now much more appreciative of the wonderful people and the beauty that usually surround me. The joy of now has returned.

A Passing Kindness

A tsunami of exhaustion engulfed me. I had failed to observe the stop sign on the road to overdoing things and was paying the price. I was talked out and peopled out! In a desperate effort to recover, I was having a late, late breakfast to give time for my soul to catch up. But my mind was too jaded to respond to these belated efforts. My mind was as flat and burnt out as my body. Would I ever rise again? The lines of a Shelley poem swam into my muddled head:

> I could lie down like a tired child,
> And weep away the life of care
> Which I have borne, and yet must bear,—
> Till death like sleep might steal on me
> And I might feel in the warm air
> My cheek grow cold, and hear the sea
> Breathe o'er my dying brain its last monotony.

Amazing that no matter where you find yourself, a poet has been there before you! Shelley and I were walking in the same shoes, or should I say swimming in the same waters.

Then into this morass of self-pity came a knock on the door. Oh dear God! Could I answer it? Could I face another human being? The world was already too much with me. But then another inner voice instructed: 'Alice, will you for God's sake give yourself a good kick in the arse and get up and open that door.'

Outside was a total stranger, a woman with a gentle, smiling face, who thrust a paper bag into my hands and said quietly: 'Just passing by on my way from Dublin to West Cork. I want to say thank you for your books. They have enriched my life. Just a little gift in appreciation.'

'Will you come in?' I gasped in amazement. 'No, no,' she said firmly, 'the family are in the car.'

Then she was gone, swallowed up into the passing traffic.

I closed the door and stood in the hallway holding the little bag in awe. What a lovely thing to happen. I brought the bag into the *seomra ciúin* and placed it on a table by the window. I sensed that my caller was a woman who did not do things lightly. Her kindness and thoughtfulness washed away my mental fatigue. My exhaustion evaporated. I sat by the table and opened the bag. Inside, wrapped in soft white tissue paper, was something solid and with it was a card. The card said: 'Your last book *Tea and Talk* had cups on the cover and this jug matches them. It belonged to my mother who died a few months ago and it was the only piece of that special set left in her house. She would have loved you to have it to be part of your set.'

I unwrapped the jug and gasped in delight to find that the tall, elegant jug was a perfect match for my much-treasured set which up to then had only had a small cream jug.

As I ran my fingers over the jug, I thought about the woman who had once used it. What was her story? She had obviously reared a daughter who did not suppress a good impulse. That good impulse changed my day.

PART 5
Then and Now

I would have missed it all but for the
necessity of having to take a rest.

The Agony and the Ecstasy

Pregnancy is judged to be a natural process in the evolution of the human species. But for me the naturalness was at times questionable. The pregnant state and I were not entirely compatible. And that is an understatement! As a start-off, my mornings crashed in with a demand from my stomach to be rid of its contents. But after a breakneck dash to the bathroom and a futile puking session, my stomach would have a change of plan. This unfortunate state, mistakenly termed 'morning sickness', extended itself into an all-day test of endurance. Supposedly confined to the early weeks of pregnancy, it went on and on and on. Not a happy state-of-the-nation situation. My darling GP happily informed me that the least notice taken of these conditions the better. God bless him! He had not walked in these shoes.

Aligned with this strange condition came a light-headiness, which caused certain objects that should be

stationary to take to the air. This happened one sunny Sunday morning at Mass when the priest was transformed into the Ascension and rose from the altar, ascending upwards towards the church steeple. A hasty exit to fresh air was desirable, but not possible, because a queasy feeling that an earthquake was about to take place beneath the church clung me to the seat. Thankfully, the floor decided to stay put and the priest came back down onto the altar as the earthquake subsided.

Fast on the heels of these alarming experiences came a total aversion to foods that had hitherto been quite palatable. Certain smells sent my stomach into somersault spins, and I slowly turned from being master of my own destiny into a cauldron of unplanned volcanic reactions to everyday situations. Then, just as that phase slowly eased itself out of my life, in came swollen ankles, high blood pressure and exhaustion.

But the daddy of them all was the 'pregnancy itch'! This could turn a perfectly sane woman into a she-devil. And it did. My GP, who was a bit of a Gael-geóir, told me that there was an old Irish curse: '*Go mbeidh tochas gan ionga ort chun an tochas a scríobhadh*', which means 'May you have the itch without a nail to scratch it.' Apparently in ancient times it was the most awful curse that you could inflict on your worst enemy. I could concur!

Heat exacerbates itch. So, warmth was out! out! out! Everybody around me had to acclimatise to sub-zero temperatures. Not a situation conducive to happy home conditions. This itch, for reasons best known to itself, pitched its camp on the soles of my feet, and drove me demented. The only solution was cold feet, cold bed, cold house – cold everything. I turned into the Ice Woman. Car journeys were made with my feet sticking out the window. Sometimes I feared that my long-suffering husband would be held up by the police and suspected of carrying a corpse to be buried during the dead of night in the wooded corner of a remote field.

Eventually I finished up in the labour ward, which in pre-epidural days was not exactly like a therapeutic visit to a massage spa. Later, when I asked my sister, who was a midwife, why the labour ward was such a torture chamber, she cast a speculative eye over my physique and informed me: 'You do not have child-bearing hips. Better for you if you were broader across the bum. You have the lean and hungry build of the Taylors. Not good for baby bearing.' No answer to that sisterly observation!

My last – fifth – pregnancy followed the usual pattern, so I concluded that another boy was on the cards. But that didn't matter, as by then I had become aware of the miracle of the perfect baby. My only concern

was that all would be well. So when, at the conclusion of a shorter-than-usual labour, I heard the cry
of life, I quickly demanded of the midwife, 'Is he all
right?' 'She is perfect,' I was told. 'She?' I questioned in
amazement. 'Yes, a perfect baby girl.'

The labour ward lit up.

Thank Heaven for Little Girls!

On the first day
Of the new year
You were born.
Perfect and beautiful,
Ahead of schedule
But complete.
The agony
Of labour pains
Climaxing
In the joy
Of perfection achieved.
A little girl
The crowning glory
Tears unrestrained
Poured on your
Downy head.
You were baptised
In streams of joy.

A Time to Write

Walking in the main door of Eason's in O'Connell Street, Dublin, I came to a standstill. Right there in front of me was a large stand stacked high with copies of just one book: my book. There were hundreds of copies of *To School Through The Fields*, my very first book. It was a magic moment. I felt the thrill from the top of my head to the tips of my toes. I was delighted for me. But also for Steve MacDonagh of Brandon Books. Steve had started and nurtured his small publishing company, facing many challenges over the years, and this successful publication was a great boost to Brandon Books.

But this was about more than Steve and me. This book was about the lives of other people, ordinary people who in their own estimation had done nothing extraordinary. But they had. They had worked the land and kept the soul of rural Ireland alive during hard times. Many of them had been forced to emigrate, but had sent back financial help to their struggling families. And now *To School Through The Fields* would eventually

To Gabriel

This book could never have seen the light of day but for your loving kindness

Alice

26-5-88.

To School Through The Fields

find its way to them, retelling their own story. This book was a celebration of their lives. I felt like climbing on top of the pile of books and dancing a jig for all of us. At long last I had achieved what had been at the back of my mind for years.

I have always loved writing. From my early years I had felt the need to transfer happenings onto paper. It was as if once written down and recorded, things were safe and would not disappear. I had no big plan, but somehow felt that when the time was right things would evolve. Eventually the time came to write more extensively.

Steve, with his publisher's nose for an untold story, sensed the potential and when he rang me with the news that he wanted to publish my manuscript I danced around the kitchen. The day the first copy arrived was also a cause for dancing! Gay Byrne gave me the ear of the nation and of all the people who had lived the same life as mine in rural Ireland. Those listeners recognised *To School Through The Fields* as *their* story. Soon afterwards Steve called to my home and told me, 'Our book is top of the bestsellers' list', and I had to ask him what exactly did that mean?

That first book led to many wonderful moments for which I am extremely grateful. *To School Through The Fields* opened the door and then the story continued. For me, the day that the first copy of any book arrives is still a very special day. Up to then it has all been just a dream, but on the day you hold the first copy in your hands the dream becomes reality.

But the greatest moments of all are when I meet readers or receive letters from people who tell me that my books have brought joy into their lives. Because in the heel of the hunt, that is what life is all about.

From There
to Here

A beautiful moment experienced and savoured to the full will be recorded on the back pages of your mind. It can be reread and relived again and again. Poets do this for themselves and others. We all have our favourite poets who do it for us. How often have you read a poem and you are enthralled by the picture the poet paints. It could be a scene that you had forgotten and he or she brings it right back into your mind. They have been there. They have once stood where you are now. Their feelings are yours. Maybe it is one good reason for memorising poems – in life you may come on something quite wonderful that is beyond your word power to describe and the words of a poem from away back float into your mind. How wonderful. For many people Wordsworth's poem on daffodils is the best example of this:

… For oft, when on my couch I lie

In vacant or in pensive mood,
They flash upon that inward eye
Which is the bliss of solitude;
And then my heart with pleasure fills,
And dances with the daffodils.

Wordsworth's recall while reclining on his couch have given pleasure to many down through the years. In this way the blissful moments of others can enrich us and open our eyes to the beauty that surrounds us. And don't you love Robert Louis Stevenson's childhood sentiment:

The world is so full of a number of things,
I'm sure we should all be as happy as kings.

I'm not so sure about the happiness of kings! But it was the child's perception of a king's world. His lines would indeed make one wonder as to why we are not all dancing with happiness.

Down through the years poets have brought us into their experiences. There are times when poetry is far more appealing to read than prose. It can somehow capture an experience in a nutshell. Poets give the reader a key into their minds.

A beautiful piece of music has the same effect. It dances into your mind and, through the performer, swirls you into the world of the composer. Unlike poetry, this is a three-piece experience and it works when each one is in harmony with the other. You glide onto another level. How often has a piece of music carried you to a place long-forgotten? It can be a great feeling. To bring the past into the now. Sometimes if I hear a favourite piece of music on the radio I dance to it around the kitchen. It brings joy to now.

But sometimes if you are not in the now, a beautiful experience may pass you by almost unnoticed. One part of your mind may note it and later you may recall your lack of mindfulness with regret. A few years ago there was an oil spill out at sea and we went very early one morning to check for oiled birds on the beach. There were none. It was a breathtakingly beautiful morning, but for some reason I was not fully present. There was something else that I cannot now even remember that was occupying my mind.

Then
Early spring morning,
Nobody on the beach.
We came searching
For oiled birds.
And found only
Sparkling sunbeams
Riding bareback

On leaping waves.
A sunlit world
Alive with sea music.
It was a picture
To be painted
When the scene was fresh;
I cannot
Now recall
All the magic
That was then.

I had allowed that golden moment to pass me by.

My first experience of ballet provided a never-to-be-forgotten moment. As a child I remember admiring wonderful pictures of Margot Fonteyn in a magazine. She brought to mind a bird in flight – this is something we witnessed daily all around us in the countryside.

Many years later I was on holiday with my daughter in Boston and she booked tickets for *Romeo and Juliet* performed by the Boston Ballet. It was mesmerising. The movement, the colour and magic were unforgettable. I was spellbound. That night opened the door into subsequent memorable ballet experiences.

Even when you are in deep pain a shared beautiful experience can leave a lasting memory-print on your mind. Once I attended a performance of *The*

Nutcracker with a beloved sister whose time on earth was limited, and that evening was a treasured memory long after she was gone. On another occasion, while deep in grief, I visited the Musée d'Orsay in Paris and there stood in front of a painting by an impressionist artist of a windswept figure in a snowstorm. It was a beautiful, bleak picture of someone lost and lonely in a frozen storm. As I stood there, the picture reached out and encompassed me. The artist, though long gone, was there with me. His picture brought me comfort. There are no time barriers in creativity.

But the art of creativity is not confined to writing, painting and music. It stretches into many other fields of life. The deep satisfaction derived from baking is captured beautifully in a poem by Brendan Kennelly which was inspired by the memory of his mother making a cake. If Brendan got joy from writing the poem, how much more did his mother get from the actual cake-making that inspired it? It was probably her exuded pleasure that prompted his poem.

When we are deeply engrossed and completely focused on the creation of anything, no matter how ordinary, like gardening, wood carving, knitting or sewing, we are satisfying a creative need that is deep within us all. Nothing satisfies the mind like the fulfilling of that creative need. It brings us into the deep joy of now.

Refeathering
the Nest

The fledglings are reared and have flown the nest and your best friend may have gone on ahead of you into the great unknown. You are home alone. The family nest, once a hive of activity is now strangely quiet. After a period of readjustment, contemplation and assessment you come to the conclusion that you need to get your act together. A change of direction is required. Your mind needs to shift gear from your previous role to whatever may evolve. Life is about enjoying the rest of the journey not arriving at the destination.

You are at a crossroads, with different roads stretching out around you in various directions. And, to quote Robert Frost, you would like to 'take the road less travelled' and hopefully it might make all the difference.

But first a big decluttering needs to take place. There is a theory in life: 'Tidy your house, tidy your

mind.' It is now time to put that theory to the test.

When the fledglings fly the nest they take no luggage with them. It is all left at base camp and eventually you realise that they have no notion of coming back to collect. Their clutter is now your problem. If your partner in their rearing was into minimalist living you are lucky, and if not you now have a double whammy with which to contend. So clearing the clutter is first on the agenda.

When you are about to make a long journey into the unknown you need a guide for the journey to enable you to arrive at your desired destination. In this case a decluttered house is the desired destination. A book on how to achieve this is a necessary requirement. Otherwise you are setting out on your journey with no sense of direction and no specific destination in mind. What you need is a 'rules of the road' book to guide you. There are a lot of books on this subject, but you need the best. And the best, in my opinion, is *Spark Joy* by Marie Kondo. Now, Marie Kondo is a tough taskmaster but she will set you on course.

A decluttering journey is mentally and physically exhausting, and not without its agonising moments of remembrances and indecision. But Marie is an expert and she gives you the coping tools that guide you through all kinds of dilemmas. It will take time and patience, but eventually you *will* get there.

Your house, after a long, dedicated haul of sorting, clearing and recycling, is clear of clutter … well *almost* and a fresh wind of change blows through your home and through your mind. You discover that the 'clear your clutter and clear your mind' maxim is indeed true! Your house can breathe more freely and so can you. That's the house done, but now, what about you? You now have more time on your hands than you ever had. So what to do with it?

Of course, we could all cod ourselves into believing that we are very busy – busy doing nothing! But that is not the aim of the game. The children don't need an appendage to their lives. They now have their own lives and we need a new direction. There are many doors open and we must choose carefully as there are no endless years stretching ahead of us, and we want to appreciate and enjoy those that are left.

When faced with this situation I did a mental survey. What are the things that I put on hold while having other priorities in life? Over the years there were many pursuits that I might have enjoyed but at the time, out of necessity, they had to be sidelined. So now, like Fagan, this is the 'time to think it out again'.

Now is the time!

It Takes so Long
to Say Goodbye

They have had it. There is no more in them. They have given it their all. And they are falling asunder. Yesterday part of a heel came away. Their day has finally come. They and I have done a lot of living together and they show it. And if the truth be told, so do I. But when my time comes I will be boxed up and shoved into the ground. No choice. Which is no bad thing.

But I am forced to toll the bell for my dear old friends. This is boot euthanasia. It seems so thankless after their long years of service. I owe them a lot. They and I have shared great times and now it's time to say goodbye. But I do not want to part with them. We have been together for such a long time. A marriage made in heaven. We have had such good days walking in so many places. We originally came together for gardening and walking the woods. While climbing hilly slopes they lovingly took care of me underfoot, and massaged my toes and ankles. A warm love affair kindled. A relationship that is far more long-lasting than a sudden flare of passion that might soon burn itself out. These friends have gone far and away beyond their original call of duty. Polished up, they sneaked into posh shops and top-class hotels, where more elegant-looking footwear is the norm. Elegant footwear may look good, but often is not kind to fragile feet – though I am very impressed by ladies who balance on clifftop high heels and master the precarious art of walking in them.

As we grow older and hopefully wiser, undesirable passengers, like corns and callouses, cling like barnacles to the underside of the carrier and become part of the cargo. My old friends softly encircled them all in their embrace. They were infinitely accommodating to any painful condition that came to live with me, shielding me from their worst efforts. They were loving and caring in all circumstances and situations. True and trusted friends. Once I slipped into them, I was assured of a relaxed and comfortable journey. Surely such faithful service deserved a just reward? How would I say a gentle goodbye to them? What would I do with my faithful old boots? Could they continue in another format? How about reincarnation for old boots? Do I believe in reincarnation? Why not!

Maybe my old friends and I do not have to part, after all. Why not fill them up with lovely soft compost and plant them with wild-flower seeds? Our roles will have changed. Up to now they were the carers and now it is my time to care for them. Gradually they will soften and slowly fade away, and eventually become part of the earth, as will I. We need never say goodbye.

Both Sides Now

Yesterday in the garden I remembered her. When her husband died suddenly she came to stay with us. It was supposed to be short-term, but she stayed until she died fourteen years later. 'Never grow old, my dear,' she warned me in her precise, articulate Anglo Irish accent. 'It's an appalling condition.' She issued this proclamation one day as she slowly climbed the stairs.

But she handled her 'appalling condition' with the expertise of a skilled boatman brilliantly manoeuvring a voyage through troubled waters and avoiding as many rocks and rapids as possible. Like Oscar Wilde, she believed that the most unforgivable offence in life was to be boring, and she never fell into that trap. Her quicksilver, enquiring mind kept life around her full of vibrancy. But it was this active mind that sometimes became irritated by the limitations of her less active body.

During the fourteen years that she spent with us, she taught me many valuable lessons. One was 'Never

indulge in self-pity, it destroys you and annihilates other people.' Another was: 'There is nothing more boring that other people's operations and grandchildren.' And the final one was: 'If you put up with too much, you get too much to put up with.'

Yesterday in the garden I remembered her. Like her, I am now slowing down – or should I say *having* to slow down. But yesterday in the garden I discovered that that too has its compensations. A few years ago I would have come into this garden in the early morning and worked here all day, stopping only to eat. Now, not so. Not so!

Yesterday morning I came out full of enthusiasm to spray my roses. Roses are beautiful but demanding ladies, and mine are blighted with black spot. A few weeks ago I was at a talk by Dermot O'Neill and he cast forth a gem of wisdom: mix a tablespoon of baking soda and a tablespoon of Phostrogen in a gallon of water and spray regularly, having first cleaned around the base and fed the roses well.

By the time all this was achieved I was whacked! It was time to sit and recover. So I brought out my lunch and afterwards sat and sat and sat ... The sun was shining and the birds were singing. When you sit quietly in the garden, after a certain amount of time the birds decide that you are part of the garden furniture or a new shrub. They resume their normal activity.

Beside me the bare branches of Uncle Jacky's apple tree became a flutter of activity. Some birds flitted from feeder to feeder, others perched on the side of the little black skillet pot full of rainwater and dipped in their tiny beaks. Also hanging off the branches are three small copper pots that I had got tired of polishing and had turned into watering wells for the birds. Not until you sit and watch them, do you realise how much water birds drink. As they flew around, they chirped and sang. They were a delight to hear and to watch.

Suddenly a movement caught my eye. It was on the rose bush at the top of stone steps beside the tree. Up there, partly hidden by rambling roses, is a nesting box in the shape of a caravan. This was a gift from a bird-loving friend and because I could not pin it to the high stone wall with all the other nesting boxes I had put it up there, safe from visiting cats. Thorny roses are a great deterrent to climbing cats. Last spring it remained unoccupied.

Now as I watched, a little bird known to me as a 'Jacky Black Cap' landed on a rose branch and cocked a wary eye around him – I decided it was a 'he'. Then he hopped onto another twig a little bit closer to the circular hole of the box. Then a little bit closer, always with an observant eye. Then he disappeared inside. I could hear a regular pecking sound from within. He

was getting his home ready for a new nest. Then he emerged and flew away. Shortly afterwards another arrived. At least, I think it was another. They looked identical and as I am no Derek Mooney I did not know the difference. However, I hoped that I had a male and female moving in and planning a family in their new home. Then while the second arrival was hovering around the branches, back came the other one, so that confirmed my hopes that I had a nesting pair. They proceeded to fly back and forth, becoming gradually more relaxed as they established their ownership of their new home. As I sat watching them, a robin landed in the bird bath slightly to my left and proceeded to give herself a good shower. She merrily swished water in all directions and then took off with a flutter of sparkling wings.

At nesting time, the garden is a delightful place to be. But yesterday I would have missed it all but for the necessity of having to take a rest.

Also from Alice Taylor

**'A delightful evocation of Irishness and of the
author's deep-rooted love of the very fields of home.'**
Publishers Weekly

Alice Taylor's classic account of growing up in the Irish countryside. The biggest-
selling book ever published in Ireland, beautifully reproduced with photographs
from Alice's life.

If ever a voice has captured the colours, the rhythms, the rich, bittersweet emo-
tions of a time gone by, it is Alice Taylor's. Her tales of childhood in rural Ireland
hark back to a timeless past, to a world now lost but ever and fondly remembered.
The colourful characters and joyous moments she offers have made *To School
through the Fields* an Irish phenomenon, and have made Alice herself the country's
most beloved author.

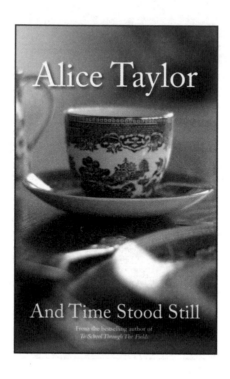

'You would have to have a heart of stone to not be moved by it.'
Arena, RTÉ Radio 1

Alice has known, loved, and lost many people throughout her life. Here she talks
about her special people, her memory of what meant so much to her about them.
She remembers her husband, father and mother, a beloved sister, her little brother
Connie, and many others. She tells how she coped with the emptiness she felt
when they died, of the seeming impossibility of moving on with life after such
deeply felt loss, when time stood still.

When we experience grief, sharing in someone else's story can help us more than
anything, and in the hands of master storyteller Alice Taylor, we may find our own
solace and the space to remember our own special people.

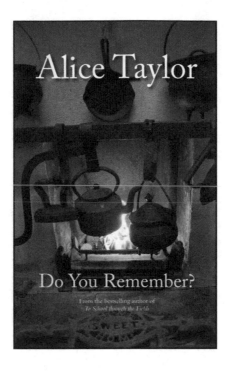

'Magical ... Reading the book, I felt a faint ache in my heart ...
It is essential reading.' *Irish Independent*

Alice Taylor remembers her childhood home – the farm with its tools and animals,
the home with its equipment for living, its daily challenges, constant hard work,
and its comforts too.

She describes the huge open fireplace where all the cooking was done, where the
big black kettle hung permanently from the crane over the flames. Here the family
sat in the evenings, talking, knitting, going over the events of the day, saying the
rosary. She recalls the faithful, beloved horses and their wonderfully varied outfits;
the excitement of threshing day and the satisfaction of a good harvest. All the jobs
and tools of a way of life long gone live on in the hearts of those who were formed
by it. Alice Taylor celebrates them with love.

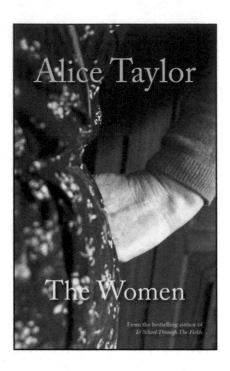

'In these pages, we see Taylor's remarkable gift of elevating the ordinary to something special, something poetic, even ... Like all of her books, it's a thing of gentle beauty.'
Irish Independent

We walk in the footprints of great women, women who lived through hard times on farms, in villages, towns and cities. The lives of these women are an untold story. This book is a celebration of the often forgotten 'ordinary' women who gave so much to our society.

Alice Taylor salutes the women whose energy and generosity made such a valuable contribution to all our lives.

'Left me feeling warm and fuzzy … I loved it from cover to cover.'
The Patricia Messinger Show, Cork's C103

See an old press overflowing with the linen collection of two generations, the oil lamps and clocks inherited and collected over many years, and the books of people who once lived here. Alice tells you of the sad loss of her beautiful dogs Kate and Lolly, friends of the heart, and takes you around her village to meet her neighbours, join a meitheal to plant trees, and visit the fairy doors in the nearby wood.

But Alice's home and community are not a perfect place: hear about the split in the local GAA club, and the donations of the local canine population on the footpaths! Visit a restored famine graveyard and hear about the landlords who once owned this village. This is life in small-town Ireland, one hundred years after the Rising.

'A must for those of you who like to put their feet up in front of the fire
and read about the joys of Christmas.'
The Kerryman

With all the warmth of a winter fire, Alice takes us through the exciting
preparation for Christmas, from getting the perfect tree to baking those crucial
puddings and pies. She gives us a intimate insight into her Christmas Eve and
Christmas day rituals and talks us through her favourite Christmas recipes. She
tells how the Christmas foods were made when she was a child, using the bastable
and the range, and how she prepares them now.

Alice loves Christmas, and her huge enjoyment of the season fills this book with
pleasure and delight.

See more books by Alice Taylor at www.obrien.ie